Charlotte Otten is Professor of English Literature (Emerita) at Calvin College, Grand Rapids, Michigan, USA. She is the author of a number of critical articles, the most recent being on women's prayers in childbirth in 16th–century England. She is Editor of *A Lycanthropy Reader: Werewolves in Western Culture* and of *English Women's Voices, 1540—1700,* which contains a compelling array of literature by women who wrote in the 16th and 17th centuries. Her poems have appeared in many journals including *Southern Humanities Review, Interim, The South Florida Poetry Review,* and the *Anglican Theological Review.* She has written a book of poems for children, *Months* which will appear in 1994. She lives in Michigan.

D0048216

THE VIRAGO
BOOK OF

Birth Poetry

EDITED BY
CHARLOTTE OTTEN

Published by VIRAGO PRESS Limited, November 1993
20-23 Mandela Street, Camden Town, London NW1 0HQ

Acknowledgements for all copyright material are given
on pages 193–203, which constitute an extension of
this copyright page

A CIP catalogue record for this title
is available from the British Library

Printed in Great Britain

In memory of my mother
Anna De Beer Fennema
(1899–1991)

Contents

3. Birthing *'She's crowning, someone says'*

4. Male Participation *'Still on my wrist I feel*
The reddish fluid
Where the waters breaking fell.'

5. The Sacred Condition *'What sacred pattern, leaping from time's loom,*
Breaks, for the opulence of the breast to feed?'

6. Miscarriage and Abortion *'There are no coffins for what is not born'*

Introduction

In the 1920s and 1930s, when my mother and my aunts were pregnant regularly, no one would have thought of writing poems about being pregnant. Even prose would have been unthinkable. These women were mildly embarrassed by their pregnancies. An aunt carried a newspaper whenever she answered the doorbell, dropping it over her protruding abdomen (she would never have used the word 'belly') to hide what was obvious. My mother stopped going to church by the fifth month of pregnancy, even though the fertile woman was praised by the official male church.

That doesn't mean that women didn't talk about pregnancy. They did. They established pregnancy networks. The newly-pregnant talked to the frequently-pregnant. The about-to-give-birth asked for advice from those whose experiences with labour were legendary. They shared attitudes towards pregnancy and childbirth. For them pregnancy was sometimes risible – a condition they could laugh about, for all its quirkiness and predictability; was sometimes indecent – they all possessed a guilty knowledge of how babies were conceived; was sometimes tragic – if the doctor had told them not to have more children and fears dominated the nine-month stretch toward death; was sometimes a joyful but inarticulate time – the long-awaited birth became an emotionally clumsy time for the one who was known as 'a barren woman'.

Curiosity about the condition of married women neighbours surfaced on washing days, Mondays in my neighbourhood. If the telltale menstrual cloths hung on the line every month, the neighbour was not pregnant. If, however, no cloths appeared on the line at the normal time, conclusions were quickly drawn. The absence signalled a conception: another neighbour was 'in the family way.' Word got around quickly. Neighbour women were prepared to help if help was needed in the early stages of pregnancy. They rallied round for the later stages, offering to take care of the children, to bring in meals, to do the washing.

Women understood one another, though there was nothing but oral communication between them. Birth was a landscape they travelled through together. The landscape had its obvious markers. Second-month nausea – eat soda crackers and avoid liquids. Third-month bleeding – get off your feet and call the doctor. Fifth-month swollen feet – take care of those kidneys and drink lots of water. Ninth-month countdown – keep active, avoid emotional stress, and clean the house.

Women were gluttons for details of another woman's labour. In the days before psychoprophylactic exercises and male participation in the birth process, in the days when most babies were born at home, husbands waited in the kitchen, if they were home at the time. Some husbands missed the birth because they were at work. Once my father came home from his long commute and found my newborn sister in the crib. There was, however, a breed of husbands who insisted upon watching while the doctor or midwife attended. Those were the husbands who could provide intimate details to women neighbours and female relatives. I remember my uncle coming to give his own graphic description of my aunt's labour, including the colour of the umbilical cord. My mother didn't want us children to hear those details, but I hung around close enough to hear him saying, 'Then the head came through,' and I wondered, 'came through', but exactly where? We knew about birth, and we didn't.

A subject that was only whispered about was the 'unwed mother'. I didn't know what that meant until a girl came to our school and we discovered that she had no father. Rumours flew around the playground that her mother had never been married. When I asked my mother about this peculiar phenomenon, she would only say, 'Her mother's tough. She took a chance. No one knew she was having a baby, and she won't tell who the father is'. That explanation didn't stop the kids at school from yelling at her, 'Where's your father?'

As for miscarriage, women had ambivalent attitudes toward it. They said to one another, 'How far along was she?' And they worried about whether the bleeding had stopped. I think my mother had never heard of a D&C. I myself hadn't heard of abortion until I took a job in a law firm and I read of the prosecution of an abortionist who had caused the death of a woman. The descriptions, even in courtroom testimony, of what this 'butcher' had done to a woman were horrendous. Certainly no one would have considered writing poetry about these uniquely female traumas.

There was a time, in the sixteenth and seventeenth centuries, when women wrote detailed accounts of their pregnancies, childbirths, and miscarriages, but the writing was for themselves – in diaries and autobiographies – or for their daughters. Their writing on these subjects was not for publication. I discovered, when I was gathering material for my book *English Women's Voices, 1540–1700,* that women gave remarkably candid accounts of the uniquely female experience. Lady Mary Carey, for example, when pregnant with her eighth child, miscarried. She looked at the dead embryo and then grieved, in a poem, for the 'dead formless babe', which apparently aborted before its quickening. Alice Thornton's complete prose history of her own pregnancies is a construct of the female self. Each clinical detail – miscarriage, labour, breech birth, haemorrhaging, fear of barrenness – separates her from the male world and gives her a distinctly female identity. In most instances, these earlier women's voices were lost to generations following them. It was not until later centuries that some of the female voices could be heard again – in published form.

It is pointless to speculate about why women didn't write poetry about pregnancy and childbirth, miscarriage and abortion in my mother's day (or in my day, some twenty and thirty years later). Perhaps they thought it was a topic unworthy of print. Perhaps they wished to keep the process strictly female and not to expose it to the harsh world of male publication. Perhaps they were ashamed of their female bodies, and the less written about them, the better. Perhaps they felt victimised, and victims rarely contribute to their own powerlessness by telling the world about their humiliation. Whatever their reasons (and, obviously, there were multiple reasons), it was a taboo subject for publication. It took an Anne Sexton to break that taboo in the 1960s with her poem 'In Celebration of My Uterus'. Not only did she write what was considered by many (especially men) an outrageous poem on an unseemly subject, but she went on the poetry circuit and read this poem to mixed audiences. Men in audiences were heard to say, 'I wish she'd stop talking about her...' and they choked on 'uterus'. The first shock was felt 'round the world'. The after-shock came in her poem 'The Abortion'.

Sexton caused an earthquake. The male world lost its equilibrium; the female world burst into poetry. Women's bodies became the poetry. No aspect of pregnancy was considered too embarrassing, too trivial, or too private for a poem. Even women who were not poets joined in the celebration: they read the poems that affirmed and enlarged their own experiences. This anthology is a celebration of that celebration.

Poems on pregnancy divide themselves easily into stages. This anthology reflects those stages. Dreams and fears of pregnancy precede pregnancy itself, and those dreams and fears can occupy as much as a forty-year span in a woman's life. Pregnancy and childbirth follow naturally, each with its unique perceptions and responses; the physical nature of pregnancy and childbirth lies close to the spiritual aspects of both pregnancy and childbirth. Male participation comes not so much as an afterthought but as recognition of the increasingly present father in the birth process itself. The glow of pregnancy – the feeling that a woman has, at about the fifth month, that her pregnancy is larger than herself, that she is part of the earth's rhythms of moons and tides – helps to sustain her in the more uncomfortable third trimester of the pregnancy. And then there is the stark reality of miscarriage and abortion, not to be ignored, but surely not the first consideration in a *Book of Birth Poetry*. From the ages roughly of twelve to fifty-two women participate in an exclusively gendered experience. They share this experience with every woman who has ever lived. It is time that their experiences are shared in poetic form. It is time for women's voices to be heard collectively: collectively they make a powerful sound.

The poems in this anthology have helped to revolutionise poetry itself. In their poems women have shown that art is not gender-biased; that art is not restricted to one gender; that art comes alive in this new gender context. Because of these poems, women can no longer be considered the Other; the Subversive; the Alternative; the Silent. Pregnancy has become the fertile soil for poetry. Women poets have caused art to bloom in wholly new and unexpected ways. Pregnancy – no longer a topic avoided by men as unsuitable for poetry – has encouraged men to add their voices to women's. The primary language of birth can now be heard.

The first section, 'Dreams and Fears of Pregnancy', covers the range of conflicting feelings that emerge in the heart of a woman in these early stages. Glancing over just a few of the poems in this section, we see women at each end of the emotional spectrum – terrified, laughing. Terror is a common emotion in pregnancy; every woman fears the birth of a child with an abnormality, whether by genes or by chance, but Patricia McCarthy exposes the raw emotion of the mother in the clinic who discovers that her child has chromosomal abnormalities. Every woman also knows what it is to be 'late', with its accompanying ambivalence. Deborah Harding talks openly about the new at-home Quick Urine Test, the feel of blood in the shower, and the sense of loss combined with relief when her period starts. The desperation of a woman who wants a child but who has not conceived is captured by Adelle Leiblein in 'Calling to the Soul of My Unborn Child.' She speaks of her 'body emptying itself/over and over/...for the thousandth time in sweat and pleasure and joy,/and no child came of it.' Reflecting on the child who will never be born, Patricia McCarthy calls it her 'Love-Child' and grieves for the child-who-never-was. At 58, Charlotte Otten laughs-laments with the matriarch Sarah about the impossibility of conceiving a child when one is past the age of conception.

The largest section in the anthology, Section 2, 'Pregnancy', is filled with language that is ebullient, like a geyser newly spouting. The languageless have become eloquent, although their attitudes toward various aspects of pregnancy are often sharply contrasting. A number of the poets explore the subject of the origins and the appearance of the growing fetus, subjects that all pregnant women contemplate. Sandra Gilbert writes of 'the nastiness of origins' while Alicia Suskin Ostriker says, 'I cannot picture/You yet. Are you thumb-length? A fish? Have you a tail?/Are you hairy?' Mira Fish sees motherhood as 'an artist's work', and the cry of a child 'at birth, is/haiku', while Joyce Carol Oates's fetus hears 'songs and eerie music, angels' flutes'. Inside her uterus Judith Wright feels the whole universe, 'the multitudinous stars,/and coloured birds and fishes' and 'sliding continents', while Rachel Hadas's 'child in the amnio x-ray shakes her fist'. The pregnancy that goes beyond nine months tries the patience of what used to be called 'the mother-to-be'. Jeanne Murray Walker coaxes the infant to be born by giving it the advice her great grandmother gave her – 'Take your licking early, and get out' – while Audre Lorde revels in the knowledge that pregnancy is eternal; in 'Now That I Am Forever with Child', her legs are 'towers between which/A new world was passing.'

Section 3, 'Childbirth', provides as varied accounts of birth as there are individual women experiencing it. No two births are alike, even for the same woman. In the Delivery Room Linda Pastan, sweating in labour, wishes that babies would 'grow in fields;/common as beets or turnips'. Although Beth Bentley has seen cattle 'drop their young', human childbirth staggers her imagination; she asks, 'What was this uprooting, this quake?' Helen Chasin humourously describes what it's like to be in the Recovery Room: 'Diapered in hospital linen,/my public seam stitched back into secrets,/I itch and heal in my crib'. Dorothy Livesay links childbirth to music, to the movements of the earth: 'The final bolt has fallen,/The firmament is riven'. The uniqueness of the shared experience transcends all medical textbook descriptions of childbirth.

Section 4, 'Male Participation', recognises that pregnancy and childbirth have a profound impact on the male, an impact that men are now willing to make poems about. One father, George Charlton, 'pukes into the pan/Out of sympathy' for his puking wife. Robert Pack, an empathetic and slightly envious male, acknowledges that all human beings begin as female and continue as female into a certain stage of growth, when 'the testes of the male begin the secretion of testosterone'; he wants the pregnant woman to know that he feels 'a bit left out'. Accompanying his wife to buy a maternity gown, David Holbrook discovers that her pregnancy does not create a bond between husband and wife but that she separates herself from him, 'remote in [her] breeding trance, as a woman is'. R. S. Thomas, a reluctant father, admits to his child, 'It was your mother wanted you;/you were already half-formed/when I entered.' A number of male poets talk about their experiences in 'The Borning Room'. Jeremy Hooker realises that, inspite of his active presence, 'She was beyond me'. And Matt Simpson, father-poet, projects himself into the voice of the child, a 'nine pound bully boy', in whose voice he can accept responsibility for putting the mother through 'that kind of thing'. Finally, James Kirkup, providing vivid details about the sperm-donation process, reflects on his never-to-be-known children 'produced by artificial insemination'.

Section 5, 'The Sacred Condition', has a quasi-mystical sound. Yet for all that, the poems give a realistic portrait of how a woman makes the leap from her physical state to the metaphysical state that pregnancy induces. The two states co-exist amicably. Amir Gilboa sings a Hebrew song, 'Good for you, my God,/the child is caught in your net...my earth is all one piece, engraved/with the stalks of flowers,/green.' A North American Indian woman calls to the sun, 'You day-sun, circling around'. In strong metaphors, Mary McAnally blends the body of a pregnant woman with the earth: 'Her menses makes the ocean floor shift,/and tidal waves proclaim her pain.' In a pensive poem about Mother Eve, Linda Pastan argues that Eve's problem was that she had no mother. The paradox of the creation of a human being out of darkness puzzles Judith Wright, 'You who were darkness warmed my flesh/where out of darkness rose the seed.' Christmas is the time for Anne Ridler to reflect on 'the glory of the flesh'; exalting all human birth, 'Christ comes/At the iron senseless time, comes/To force the glory into frozen veins'. The Korean poet Kim Nam-Jo identifies her baby with the 'starry field of the sky,/or heap of pearls in the depth.' And, with the birth cycle coming full circle, Louise Glück pines for the days, thirty years ago, when she was still a fetus in her mother's womb because 'it was better when we were/together in one body.' John Frederick Nims cannot keep from singing about the miracle of his son's birth: 'How the greenest of what rang gold at his birth!'; the Michigan earth resonates with his joy.

Section 6, 'Miscarriage and Abortion', demonstrates that poems can be written on two highly emotional but physical topics. Some of the poems reach for ecstasy; others sink close to despair. All of the poems admit the subject into poetic consciousness, where, apart from politics, an honest portrayal of ambiguities and stresses is achieved. Nancy Willard, who wakes up 'in a wave of blood', rejoices when she hears the heartbeat of the living child and shouts, 'A thousand thumping rabbits! Savages clapping for joy!' Years after a miscarriage at home the pregnant woman in Ellen Wittlinger's poem broods over the embryo which she had put into a jar and which she observes looks 'like a fish'. 'In the third month,' cries Anthony Hecht, 'the frail image of God/Lay spilled and formless.' Suzette Bishop's tone is ironic: 'Doctors Are Solving the Mystery of Miscarriage'. With clinical detail she outlines the 'evacuation' process in a miscarriage: 'Considerable progress demystifying Enduring six miscarriages/was almost too much to bear. Empty.' David Galler recalls how, in 1952 in Greenwich Village, an abortionist came into their apartment and performed the abortion, 'Blood all over the floor...The foetus dried on the stove.' His staged detachment gives the poem its poignancy. In Ai's poem, 'the fetus [is] wrapped in wax paper'. For those among us who have never had a miscarriage or an abortion, the poems bring us into direct contact with those who have. For a few moments their anguish, their uncertainty, their pain is ours.

Each poet in this anthology has headed straight into uncharted territory. The freshness of discovery is there. No long, carefully charted, tradition intrudes or commands. *The Virago Book of Birth Poetry* has blazed its own trail. All who come after will see the prints of those who have travelled here before.

Finding poems for this collection was an exciting, and sometimes frustrating, task. Some of the most exciting times occurred in libraries that have extensive holdings in journals of contemporary poetry. I browsed through hundreds of journals from 1970 on, always hoping to discover another voice on the subject. When I did, I wanted to shout. Next came reading books of poems; reading the Table of Contents was often not enough. Titles can be deceptive, or not evocative enough to indicate the content of the poems. The bonus for me was that I read a lot of poetry. I began to realise that many contemporary poets were female. Again, I wanted to shout. Finally, I checked with my friends who were poets. Several of them had written poems that would fit into the anthology – and they were delighted to be discovered.

Selecting poems for this anthology was probably more frustrating than exciting. Excluding poems is difficult. I re-read all the poems and then made the painful decisions. I had to keep constant check on my criteria. Selecting the poems took more time than I had bargained for. Although I did not deliberately try for a multicultural mix, I discovered that I had one. My final selection included poets from Chile, Australia, New Zealand, Korea, Jamaica, Belgium, as well as from the United States, Canada, and Great Britain. I also discovered that I had an ethnic mix: Welsh, Irish, Asian, Black, Hispanic, Native American. Birth makes neither cultural nor ethnic distinctions.

Having completed the selection process, I was ready for the permissions process. All excitement was gone. Not quite. Encouragement along the way came in the form of letters attached to signed permissions forms. One poet called me 'brave' for undertaking this anthology and sent along a clutch of her poems that moved me to tears. Another sent two books of her own poems (that were out-of-print and hard to come by) – poems that I read as soon as they arrived because they were so compelling. The frustration grew into disappointment when the cost of permission fees exceeded my budget. Some poems could not be included because I couldn't afford them. Then there were the poets who seemed to have left no trace of their whereabouts. I simply couldn't find them, even after sleuthing.

The Virago Book of Birth Poetry does not contain all the poems that have been written within the last thirty years on the subject. It is a beginning. I hope each reader murmurs, as she reads in the anthology, 'I wish Charlotte Otten had included...' Then the book will have accomplished what it set out to do: to evoke responses, conversation, dialogue. And ultimately more poetry.

I want to thank all the poets who made their poems available for this book. I am happy to be the one who brought them together. Together the poems change the contours of pregnancy, childbirth, miscarriage and abortion.

Charlotte Otten
1993

1

Dreams and Fears of Pregnancy

'The girl dreams milk within her body's field'

Anne Sexton

IN CELEBRATION OF MY UTERUS

Everyone in me is a bird.
I am beating all my wings.
They wanted to cut you out
but they will not.
They said you were immeasurably empty
but you are not.
They said you were sick unto dying
but they were wrong.
You are singing like a school girl.
You are not torn.

Sweet weight,
in celebration of the woman I am
and of the soul of the woman I am
and of the central creature and its delight
I sing for you. I dare to live.
Hello, spirit. Hello, cup.
Fasten, cover. Cover that does contain.
Hello to the soil of the fields.
Welcome, roots.

Each cell has a life.
There is enough here to please a nation.
It is enough that the populace own these goods.
Any person, any commonwealth would say of it,
'It is good this year that we may plant again
and think forward to a harvest.
A blight had been forecast and has been cast out.'
Many women are singing together of this:
one is in a shoe factory cursing the machine,
one is at the aquarium tending a seal,
one is dull at the wheel of her Ford,
one is at the toll gate collecting,
one is tying the cord of a calf in Arizona,
one is straddling a cello in Russia,
one is shifting pots on the stove in Egypt,

one is painting her bedroom walls moon color,
one is dying but remembering a breakfast,
one is stretching on her mat in Thailand,
one is wiping the ass of her child,
one is staring out the window of a train
in the middle of Wyoming and one is
anywhere and some are everywhere and all
seem to be singing, although some can not
sing a note.
Sweet weight,
in celebration of the woman I am
let me carry a ten-foot scarf,
let me drum for the nineteen-year-olds,
let me carry bowls for the offering
(if that is my part).
Let me study the cardiovascular tissue,
let me examine the angular distance of meteors,
let me suck on the stems of flowers
(if that is my part).
Let me make certain tribal figures
(if that is my part).
For this thing the body needs
let me sing
for the supper,
for the kissing,
for the correct
yes.

Gabriela Mistral

MOTHER

My mother came to see me; she sat right here beside me,
and, for the first time in our lives, we were two sisters
who talked about a great event to come.

She felt the trembling of my belly and she gently uncovered
my bosom. At the touch of her hands to me it seemed as if
all within me half-opened softly like leaves, and up into
my breasts shot the spurt of milk.

Blushing, full of confusion, I talked with her about my
worries and the fear in my body. I fell on her breasts,
and all over again I became a little girl sobbing in her
arms at the terror of life.

Translated by Langston Hughes

Anne Stevenson

'BIRTH'

Birth.
Impossible to imagine
not knowing how to expect.

Childbirth.
Impossible to imagine
years of the tall son.

Death.
Impossible to imagine,
exactly, exactly.

Linda Nemec Foster

THE PREGNANT WOMAN DREAMS OF HERSELF

I am naked and lost.
There is no hope of finding me
unless you are willing to climb
the mountain of clear glass
that tricks your eye
with changing colors;
that cuts your feet
like crystal knives;
that deceives you with blank
mirrors, promises of help;
that lies about the distance
to the top. Sooner or later
you will discover this wild
prism, this trapped rainbow.
Slowly, you will begin the climb.

Jorie Graham

WANTING A CHILD

How hard it is for the river here to re-enter
the sea, though it's most beautiful, of course, in the waste
of time where it's almost
turned back. Then
it's yoked,
trussed...The river
has been everywhere, imagine, dividing, discerning,
cutting deep into the parent rock,
scouring and scouring
its own bed.
Nothing is whole
where it has been. Nothing
remains unsaid.
Sometimes I'll come this far from home
merely to dip my fingers in this glittering, archaic
sea that renders everything

identical, flesh
where mind and body
blur. The seagulls squeak, ill-fitting
hinges, the beach is thick
with shells. The tide
is always pulsing upward, inland, into the river's rapid
argument, pushing
with its insistent tragic waves – the living echo,
says my book, of some great storm far out at sea, too far
to be recalled by us
but transferred
whole onto this shore by waves, so that erosion
is its very face.

Laurie Lee

MILKMAID

The girl's far treble, muted to the heat,
calls like a fainting bird across the fields
to where her flock lies panting for her voice,
their black horns buried deep in marigolds.

They climbed awake, like drowsy butterflies,
And press their red flanks through the tall branched grass,
and as they go their wandering tongues embrace
the vacant summer mirrored in their eyes.

Led to the limestone shadows of a barn
they snuff their past embalmèd in the hay,
while her cool hand, cupped to the udder's fount,
distils the brimming harvest of their day.

Look what a cloudy cream the earth gives out,
fat juice of buttercups and meadow-rye;
the girl dreams milk within her body's field
and hears, far off, her muted children cry.

Deborah Harding

LATE

I'm holding my urine for the Quick Test
starting to believe it's possible,
small bud of my child,
my half a thumb, is it you?
Every half hour I've been checking
for blood, slipping my hand under the sheet,
quick touch at the velvet opening,
the place where the head would crown.
On the bed, a block of moonlight,
my husband's bare legs.
I flick on the tiny book light
not to wake him, nothing.
At six I pour my pee in a vile,
little perfume sampler, mix in the clear,
maybe it's blue, maybe not.
Stepping into a steaming shower
I think I feel something, that inevitable red
sloughed in my hand, a prayer
stripped from my lips, and in those first
drops, the egg is lost — in the wet
curve of my palm
a tiny shard of her, glistening,
translucent as the beginning of a tear.

Kathleen Fraser

POEM WONDERING IF I'M PREGNANT

Is it you? Are you there,
thief I can't see,
drinking,
leaving me at the edge
of breathing?
New mystery floating up my left arm,

clinging to the curtain.
    Uncontrollable.
Eyes on stalks, full of pollen,
stem juice, petals making ready to unfold,
to be set in a white window,
or an empty courtyard.
Fingers fresh. And cranium,
    a clean architecture
    with doors
        that swing open...
is it you, penny face?
Is it you?

Faye Kicknosway

IN MYSTERIOUS WAYS

Condoms keep catching at the river's
skirt. And some girl, swimming
in New Jersey – a virgin who doesn't know what
it's all about, has no explanation
for anything – gets bitten
on her trunks by one of them
that's filled out
like a little fish. And it's a Miracle
a *real* Miracle,
what pops her belly out.
But no one
believes her; no one.

Linda Taylor

TRYING TO HAVE CHILDREN WITH THE WRONG MAN

When chickens don't get enough grit,
their eggs get soft and rot.
Though still broody and fierce,
the hens begin to eat them up.
I dreamed of having another embryo
slide red, too soon, from between my legs:

Raising from its flat envelope
was a pale head, with sweet, closed eyes.
I put its face to my breast, imagined
there would be no milk, but there was,
a slurping sound, a pull inside, and white
running from the corners of its mouth.

Like a doll it lay, sweet, content,
until, bodiless, its little milky
head bobbed aside showing white
through empty eyes filled up with milk.
One ought to listen to something saying, 'No,
this isn't to be,' and not stick, against advice.

This March is a hard, birthing month,
not sentimental breezes, but touch
and go, between life and death, the blue
murderous to even half-unfolded
flesh, the sap risen, desirous,
color crumbling from the sky.

Failing flesh, we may make substance
of desire, the stone bleeding red,
the sun revealed, each day from nothing; looking up,
for a hole in the sky, for the painful
moment when the child comes out,
face down, into the light.

Charlotte Otten

FETAL STONE

A friend dreamed I had given birth.
At 58? What live again?
Sarah laughing at God's visitors,
Angels chasing wind,
Aborted fetal stone.

The oak outside my window
Tells the truth. The spruce trees lie.
I shall not bear a child as spruce
Bear snow to heaven, a sacrifice in white,
But like the bloody oak, marooning to the sky,
Delivering birth to earth,
I am now most alive

Because I die.

Toi Derricotte

THIS WOMAN WILL NOT BEAR CHILDREN

men might put their hands
on my belly &
feel the awful roar of seven oceans

i might fit my fullness
into them

but my mother warned me

i am not tempted
to tear the cloth
& fray those spindly nerves
tucked in tender lobes

she soothed them with her voice
crooned them to sleep
     though
i long for that electric spill
pole to pole
two vacuums sucking one light

death is protection

kiss me on my lips
i would wake

Elizabeth Jennings

THE UNKNOWN CHILD

That child will never lie in me, and you
Will never be its father. Mirrors must
Replace the real image, make it true
So that the gentle love-making we do
Has powerful passions and a parents' trust.

The child will never lie in me and make
Our loving careful. We must kiss and touch
Quietly, watch our own reflexions break
As in a pool that is disturbed. Oh take
My watchful love; there must not be too much.

A child lies within my mind. I see
the eyes, the hands. I see you also there.
I see you waiting with an honest care,
Within my mind, within me bodily,
And birth and death close to us constantly.

Adelle Leiblein

CALLING TO THE SOUL OF MY UNBORN CHILD

I began it when the reign of our flesh
failed to bring us a child,
after years of my body emptying itself
over and over, the way the sky goes colorless
after the biggest storm of the year, a huge blank eye,
after I had learned the purpose behind all the tables
of how the needle swings, the deep bowel gurgles,
how the body sings a litany of curious cravings.
I began it when all my female parts clamped down
for the thousandth time in sweat and pleasure and joy,
and no child came of it.

I began it when I had searched the face of my husband
who was searching mine for some slight shadow,
some mild betrayal, for some vague, soft holding back.
I began it after I'd been warned by the roundness of pain,
been stuck with bleeding that goes unstaunched;
I began it when I had no other choice.

I take a book down off a shelf, I put it back again.
Waking from sleep I half-hear a fragment of my husband's mumble
as he drops off, '...love you,'
confirming in two words more than I deserve.
I do it when I'm alone in our house and say,
'When my child is my age it will be nineteen hundred and...'
knowing I must now rephrase.
I do it when I dream my lover a dowser
and myself a silver strand just below the surface.
I do it when I wear black on black,
matching mode to mood, strong with power and resolve,
dark as the deepest soil, coal about to be diamond.

Once, before lovemaking, I filled our room with lit candles,
laid out heaps of marigold petals and rice,
small plates of milk around the bed,
attar of roses on the pillows.

In the meantime, sweet husband asked,
'Would it help if I believed?' – an offering
in the face of all this daunting, amalgamated hope.
I couldn't bear to answer no or yes.

I will do it knowing as I do
that wanting one man is dangerous,
wondering if wanting more than one is inevitable,
knowing that I am not the old dry wife,
but a sweet plowed acre...
I will do it because I know the discrepancy
between what we want and what we have.
I will do it in a hundred different guises,
more because of hope than of habit.

I will do it until I'm talked-out, wordless,
'til my child will hear me and move through that scrim,
between this world and elsewhere,
until conditions of the universe are harmonious
and the child will come in me, and slip into her skin,
come in nakedness, breathing, rosey, and whole,
come to share with us this life on earth.

Patricia McCarthy

LOVE-CHILD

Child whom I'll never carry,
I'd like you. You'd be a girl,
I think, a lefthanded knockout:
no sin, our only ours.

He who'll never be your father:
one of three, three in one –
is kind and wouldn't insult you
with condemnation. The cradle

of his smile rocks beautifully –
with rowan leaves to protect you
from evil and abracadabras
in its corners in tiny triangles.

I've slid and slid down his body
arching over me your rainbow,
testing it for safety. As we wring
birth from death, death from birth –

unfair on you, he doesn't know
I've conceived you already by
embracing a May-tree and Saint
Swithin swells me like an apple

with the rain. You can perch
on his palm, a Thumbelina, while
I fashion a caul from my webs
that will give you lyres –

so it's said and lovers for
the choosing. I'm avoiding
strawberries in case of markings
and touching wood for you

at every boasting. You need
more advantages than most.
You thrill my belly over all
the humpbacked bridges I cross

to him too fast, wavering
between desire and sense, instinct
and science. If I told him now,
he'd polish an eagle-stone

for me to wear on my arm,
rattling the pebble inside it
to make you squirm, doting as much
as me. But on the verge of you

I delay, withholding drams
of spit, sperm, wine and word
to mix with you squandered flesh
into a flying ointment

for saturnalia with you —
after the french-letter, worn
delicately as a caul, thrusts
at you the tenderest No.

As hens crow in the dark, eating
their eggs, I twist our last straw
of ecstasy into a harvest-baby
and swaddle it in oblivion.

Judith Sornberger

PREPARATIONS

Thirty-six, and not a son
or daughter to her name.
Does she want one?
Her mother told her
angels bring us babies.
In her dream they flew through sunrise,
pink and blue tufts streaming
from their icy morning wings.
Aunt Jenny had no children.
Didn't the angels like her?

She lifts crystal angels
from a tissue paper cradle,
arranges them under this year's
Christmas tree — a tumbleweed.
Yes, she is tumbling, drifting…
Wasn't there something
she wanted to ask for?

She sets up the papier-mache creche
next to the angels, like dolls
under the tree, a new baby each year,
the way she thinks it must be
for women without choices.

Has she made a choice?
Or is she waiting for someone
with a beautiful name like Gabriel
to tap her on the shoulder?
She wraps the tree in white
lights and tinsel like a bride.
All night it will say 'O'
in the black window.

Miriam Pederson

EROSION

Everything is wearing thin.
The rugs, the dish towels,
our socks, this chair,
the snow.
Look at it,
worn and soiled.
It's a crime
to let things go this far.
Nothing can be done
to bring them back.
Who can remember
when patches on jeans
were important?
My mother
turned collars on shirts
to make them new again
but that is over.
There is no time

to save things anymore.
I am afraid to bear a child
with this thinness all around –
sheets that tear
when we toss in the night,
hair that falls
from our heads,
top soil that washes
from our land.
Who can know
when these shoes will wear out
and my child will walk barefoot
over what is left.

Vassar Miller

SPINSTER'S LULLABY

For Jeff

Clinging to my breast, no stronger
Than a small snail snugly curled,
Safe a moment from the world,
Lullaby a little longer.

Wondering how one tiny human
Resting so, on toothpick knees
In my scraggly lap, gets ease,
I rejoice, no less a woman

With my nipples pinched and dumb
To your need whose one word's sucking.
Never mind, though. To my rocking
Nap a minute, find your thumb

While I gnaw a dream and nod
To the gracious sway that settles
Both our hearts, imperiled petals
Trembling on the pulse of God.

Charlotte Otten

RISKING A SECOND CHILD

I never lived for chance;
eschewed all games of dice,
afraid to play with cards
whose random distribution
might threaten equanimity.

Except for *Rook*
(and that, I thought, required more skill than chance),
I would not touch a card –
those 'devil' aces, jacks, and kings and queens
that were purportedly in league
with destiny and fate,
and with an underworld that lurked in the abyss
within the soul.

You were my biggest gamble,
my blood ran toxins through your brother's veins.
Would my polluted blood kill you
before you ever saw the light of day,
or me?

Two weeks before the mortal game
that would decide my fate and yours,
you defied augury;
forced destiny and fate out of the underworld;
played the Rook card when their high trump was on the table;
swore by your live birth
that Providence made you the winner.

'In that was heaven ordinant':
From your sweet, fair, and unpolluted flesh
I saw the violets spring;
your cries sweet balm
anointing my flat belly.

Patricia McCarthy

ANTE NATAL CLINIC

A nissen hut through which other mothers to be
waddle knowledgeably, bellies ripe as fruits,
through an assured future for each pregnancy.

Unlike me, they open the free samples
of baby lotion. Theirs are the healthy infants
gurgling in Cow and Gate advertisements on the walls.

Theirs is the team of doctors and nurses who take
creation for granted; theirs – the new scanner,
the only loss – which causes no ache –

that of privacy as obstetric records are filled
semi-publicly. At least they need run no risks
because all the risks fall on me, billed

as Prima Gravadis. Though they wear gestation
like an apron, it hangs on me like the sackcloth
of a captive who, alone, realises a war is on.

Mine are the black statistics squirming, unchangeable,
into chromosomal abnormalities and Down's Syndrome
on a chart on a board. Mine the losses – irredeemable –

that pin together the lips of my interrogators.
Yet since I don't look my age, I believe, for a moment,
I shall carry you full term and become a member

of the pram club, Mothercare and playground railings,
turning my thoughts magically into stuffed animals.
I don't want you to hear about the risks of failing.

But to find a cradle carved by the wind's lullabies
while I rest in its Westerly sling, preparing to squat
for the first birth ever, measuring your size.

However, I sit where I'm told, tortured by congratulations
mistimed, staring at the blank diagnostic sheet
it's doubted I'll need, caught between despair and elation.

The other women don't turn a hair when I leave
with an inmate's number. They can't see the deformities
in my tiny ration of hope that I happened to conceive

with you. Nor do they know how, as prisoner of a war
they won't have to wage, I will you to carry on
dreaming in me that the sun will somehow restore

my hair to the veil of the perfect madonna. Making
peace, she will prepare a nursery from light.
If I'm gagged in the hut, you'll be hers for the taking.

Muriel Rukeyser

NIGHT FEEDING

Deeper than sleep but not so deep as death
I lay there dreaming and my magic head
remembered and forgot. On first cry I
remembered and forgot and did believe.

I knew love and I knew evil:
woke to the burning song and the tree burning blind,
despair of our days and the calm milk-giver who
knows sleep, knows growth, the sex of fire and grass,
renewal of all waters and the time of the stars
and the black snake with gold bones.

Black sleeps, gold burns; on second cry I woke
fully and gave to feed and fed on feeding.
Gold seed, green pain, my wizards in the earth
walked through the house, black in the morning dark.
Shadows grew in my veins, my bright belief,

my head of dreams deeper than night and sleep.
Voices of all black animals crying to drink,
cries of all birth arise, simple as we,
found in the leaves, in clouds and dark, in dream,
deep as this hour, ready again to sleep.

Richard Jones

WHITE TOWELS

I have been studying the difference
between solitude and loneliness,
telling the story of my life
to the clean white towels taken warm from the dryer.
I carry them through the house
as though they were my children
asleep in my arms.

2

Pregnancy

'I'm sore with life'

Alicia Suskin Ostriker

ONCE MORE OUT OF DARKNESS (ii)

The supposed virgins sitting in a circle
Under old portraits of Margaret Sanger
Are here to receive their first, new innocent diaphragms;
I, however, am their fabled goddess.
I am conducted to the sanctuary, I submit to indignities,
Skirt up, feet in stirrups, one look, one rotating poke –
Examination of the entrails? Quite right, due process,
My cow. 'Five weeks,' the voice intones. 'Hooray,'
I say, and pay (the dogfaced nurses cheerful)
And get to a phone fast, pretending to be
(In the shabby drugstore) Western Union, a singing telegram,
'Love, oh love, oh careless love,' it sings, 'you see
What Love has done to me,' and hang up giggling.

Consequence: Join the world, which is full
Of ballooning mamas and baffled but willing papas for future
Communion. We join it. We toss
Off quarts of milk, we invent spinach recipes
To rectify the diet, we observe the tenderness
Of my breasts, and that I pee more and sleep more
And weep more: by which signs alone is made known
The invisible change, the silent grafting-on
Or addition of an infinity, the implausible, actual
Shift of the people universe, for which we are
Responsible. Nevertheless, my foetus, I cannot picture
You yet. Are you thumb-length? A fish? Have you a tail?
Are you hairy? Will I be good to you?
Archangel Spock, Guttmacher, Grantely Dick-Read,
Pray for us now, we follow your lead.

Helena Minton

GOD, WOMAN, EGG

After 'Madonna', a lithograph by Edvard Munch

She never asked to lose innocence
like this: angels fingering her
the thrust of doves and roses at her door.
She had been soft and free.
Now the sky strikes her hair
lightning wielded by insomniacs
and her womb becomes the world's:
the foetus in one corner folded
skull and cross bones like a mouse
in a broom closet.

Each day its nails grow longer.
Sperm flow like the Jordan in her dreams.
She is God's purse, snapped tight.
She'll shrink as Jesus fattens
with her germ, elbows
the sac open and slides out, the spirit
a glue on his tiny thumbs.

Sandra M. Gilbert

ABOUT THE BEGINNING

The nastiness of origins!
When she put on that pink shantung,

she wasn't thinking of you;
straightening his tie, he was equally

indifferent. Their blind date
with your destiny was just another

dumb night out. At the restaurant,
his best friend joked that the wine

was 'unpretentious' while hers
kept visiting the ladies room

to change her Modess. The Italian waiter
scowled and limped but didn't

belong to the Mafia. Nobody
drank too much, nobody

told any interesting stories. He
thought maybe he'd seen her once or twice again.

She thought he was too skinny. She was
really stuck on a flashy

lawyer in Brooklyn and this shy
guy just had a dull job with the city.

As for you, you didn't know the difference
between yourself and any other egg.

No, you were only half a cell, stranded among
slick membranes, and when

they had married and copulated and you'd swelled
alarmingly into a body

with fingerprints intact
and you were inching out of *her* body

in short sharp jerks,
she was only thinking about the awful

pain this whole business was causing her
because she still didn't know who you were –

you with your booties and your allergies,
your sonnets and your discoveries:

you were still lighter in her thought
than the silk flower on the straw hat

she'd planned to wear on that fatal date
and then forgotten about.

Joan Rohr Myers

FERTILITY

It is now, when the whole jar
of humidity has been poured on me
like wet petals, and there is no question
of dryness anywhere, that I am most close
to everything alive: the wet breath
that links leaves and sky to my lungs
reaches deep inside my body and stirs
the silent seeds of all I hold dear,
and you, like the powerful muscle
we call heart, grow stronger within me.

Charlotte Otten

PREGNANT

The dizziness proceeds
through aural labyrinths,
gets caught on sight
rather than sound,
stumbles backward
on sandsilk stairs
bringing the universe
down on a private beach.

Arhythmic crashing
into rhythmic pulses
of moon and tides,
stars swirl
inside the womb,
a blob of blood
swims in a fish,
egg becomes yoke
within a thickening wall.

Mira Fish

PREGNANCY

yours is a benison,
the supper bone
to dogs.

You have been starved
for a child;
a miracle, your womb;
a fairy tale.

But your conception is
wrong!
He will not be born a hero,
the Christ, Good News.

Will you learn this motherhood
is an artist's work?
that the child, his cry
at birth, is
haiku?

Chana Bloch

THE SECRET LIFE

I carried the child for weeks without telling,
letting the secret
feed me. Only you and I knew
and we closed

around each other. I grew a path
we could take without needing
to speak. Light passed between us
at midnight, poured

from a cloudy source and kept
pouring. We drank
and drank and the tipped glass
refilled itself.

Anne Stevenson

THE SUBURB

No time, no time,
and with so many in line to be
born or fed or made love to, there is no
excuse for staring at it, though it's spring again
and the leaves have come out looking
limp and wet like little green new born babies.

The girls have come out in their new bought dresses,
carefully, carefully. They know they're in danger.
Already there are couples crumpled under the chestnuts.
The houses crowd closer, listening to each other's radios.
Weeds have got into the window boxes. The washing hangs,
helpless. Children are lusting for ice cream.

It is my lot each May to be hot and pregnant,
a long way away from the years when I slept by myself –
the white bed by the dressing table, pious with cherry blossoms,
the flatteries and punishments of photographs and mirrors.
We walked home by starlight and he touched my breasts.
'Please, please!' Then I let him anyway. Cars
droned and flashed, sucking at the cow parsley. Later
there were teas and the engagement party. The wedding
in the rain. The hotel where I slept in the bathroom.
The night when he slept on the floor.

The ache of remembering, bitterer than a birth. Better
to lie still and let the babies run through me.
To let them possess me. They will spare me
spring after spring. Their hungers deliver me.
I grow fat as they devour me. I give them my sleep
and they absolve me from waking. Who can accuse me?
I am beyond blame.

Joyce Carol Oates

FOETAL SONG

The vehicle gives a lurch but seems
to know its destination.
In here, antique darkness. I guess at things.
Tremors of muscles communicate
secrets to me. I am nourished.
A surge of blood pounding sweet
blossoms my gentle head.
I am perfumed wax melted of holy candles
I am ready to be fingered and shaped.

This cave unfolds to my nudge, which
seems gentle but is hard as steel.
Coils of infinite steel are my secret.
Within this shadowless cave I am not confused
I think I am a fish, or a small seal.
I have an impulse to swim, but without
moving; *she* moves and I drift after...
I am a trout silent and gilled, a tiny seal
a slippery monster knowing all secrets.
Where is she off to now? – in high heels.
I don't like the jiggle of high heels.
On the street we hear horns, drills, feel sleeves,
feel rushes of language moving by
and every stranger has possibly
my father's face.

Now we are in bed.
Her heart breathes quiet and I drink blood.
I am juicy and sweet and coiled.
Her dreams creep upon me through nightmare slots of
    windows
I cringe from them, unready.
I don't like such pictures.
Morning...and the safety of the day brings us
bedroom slippers, good.
Day at home, comfort in this sac,

three months from my birthday I dream
upon songs and eerie music, angels' flutes
that tear so stern upon earthly anger
(now they are arguing again).
Jokes and unjokes, married couple,
they clutch at each other in water
I feel him nudge me but it is by accident.
The darkness of their sacs must be slimy with dead tides
and hide what they knew of ponds and knotty ropes of
    lilies.

It forsakes them now, cast into the same bed.
The tide throws them relentlessly into the same bed.
While he speaks to her I suck marrow from her bones.
It has a grainy white taste, a little salty.
Oxygen from her tremendous lungs taste white too
but airy bubbly, it makes me dizzy...!

She speaks to him and her words do not matter.
Marrow and oxygen matter eternally. They are mine.
Sometimes she walks on concrete, my vehicle,
sometimes on gravel, on grass, on the
blank worn tides of our floors at home.
She and he, months ago, decided not to kill me.
I rise and fall now like seaweed fleshed to fish, a surprise.
I am grateful.
I am waiting for my turn.

Kirk Robertson

POSTCARD TO A FOETUS

i just thought
since you're all curled up
inside there
i'd tell you about it
how it was

when your mother & i
came together
in a moon of cherries
squirrel ran up a tree
wind blew but stopped
when the pipe was lit
& the breath was trapped
in small buckskin pouches
i was told
you will have a tough life
all you can do
is go through it
and that's how small things
survive like grass
pushes up through
cracks in the asphalt

Colette Inez

WAITING FOR THE DOCTOR

I hear the doctor's loud success
booming to the anteroom,
my convent girl legs
criss-crossed at the ankles
narrowing the chapel where love huffs
like a wolf in the gray light
of unredemptive sex.

Eucharistic body, tasty wafer,
Bristol-Cream sherry tapping through my veins,
Catholic outcome of a priest-father,
Medieval mother on the guest bed of the parish,
witnessed by an ivory angel
and a watercolor Christ.

Waiting for the doctor, his loud success,
I think: my mother's breasts at thirty
tightening in my father's palms,
a crack inside her plaster flesh
widening for life,
my infant body's instant flush.

Disgusting girl – female scum, dirty secretions
attendant on woman's time, my mother thought
tying the parcel to mail me away.
I, reared on the assembly line,
factory for molding children into nuns.
Orphanage cookie, my cookie-self

waiting for the doctor
to come and view my masterworks:
assemblages of bone, mid-symphysial stage of decay,
sculptures for love programmed to fail,
but doubling cells under my flesh humming like a
     laundromat
a 9-lb. load to cart in and out of next year's bed.

Judith Wright

THE MAKER

I hold the crimson fruit
and plumage of the palm;
flame-tree, that scarlet spirit,
in my soil takes root.

My days burn with the sun,
my nights with moon and star,
since into myself I took
all living things that are.

All things that glow and move,
all things that change and pass,
I gather their delight
as in a burning-glass;

all things I focus in
the crystal of my sense.
I give them breath and life
and set them free in the dance.

I am a tranquil lake
to mirror their joy and pain;
and all their pain and joy
I from my own heart make,

since love, who cancels fear
with his fixed will,
burned my vision clear
and bid my sense be still.

Gail Rudd Entrekin

THIS TIME

(For Benjamin)

Listen.
I will do anything:
eat two raw eggs
walk slowly under you
lie on my left side
fall into the juniper bush in the dark
give up
my ankles to salt,
men's desire,
even, at last, my own
I efface

become nothing
a waiting
a moving container
clotted with love.

So that your passage through me
will leave me hollow and confused
directionless, you having gone,

and having come,
who will you be
with your mercury eyes
pink hands flexing
unfathomable needs?

Will I know you then?
For whom shall I have bent
for whose head in my hand
hungered?

Rachel Hadas

AMNIOCENTESIS

For Joel, Eleanor, and Katherine

After the apples brought down from the country,
after the Chinese food and beer and kisses of reunion,
sleepily with what syllables are left us
we talk of death and birth,
of terror and of comfort, their equation:
grandmother dying of cancer,
baby astir in the womb.
A cockroach crawls in the beer mug.
The cat with ulcered ear
purring reaches up a paw to knead
the beard of the father-to-be

who from his fragile tower
is soon to be pulled down
to paddle in the generations' river
as far as an unfathomed blood-warm sea.
Parked for a while above the common lot,
each of us, gazing at it, either thinks
of his own mother and father or does not.
The child in the amnio X-ray shakes her fist;
and in the baby shop you tell me off,
a teddy bear, wound up, makes white womb noises –
amnio growls to soothe the savage breast
of a new creature thrust cold and wild
into such a strangely silent world.
What music will you make for her, I ask.

Mary Jo Salter

EXPECTANCY

(Japan Baptist Hospital, Kyoto)

One by one, we shuffle in
and take a quiet seat beneath
admonitory posters. Here's
Mrs. Shimoda, who, to judge from
her pink, quilted jumper appliqued
with rabbits, and a fuzzy, enormous purse
emblazoned with cartoon characters,

appears to be in some confusion
as to whether she's going to have a baby
or (a greater miracle) become one;
and here's sorrowful Mrs. Fukumoto,
who hasn't looked well in weeks. Of course
I'm guessing – I'm a newcomer here,
and as the nurse calls out each name

just a touch louder than necessary,
in a kindly, patronizing singsong,
I flinch. Thermometer under tongue,
blood pressure measured, I can clearly see
a needle creeping on the hateful scale
where serene Mrs. Oh, five months along,
checks in at less than I at two.

Yet don't I, in fact, want to feel the weight
of waiting once again? The way
(years ago) each birthday took years to arrive...
Oh to be sixteen at last, to drive,
to come home past eleven! To loosen
the hold of parents who'd grown to fear
time as a thing they only got less of,

while you knew, yourself, it was stored within.
Too early, I know, I begin to imagine
how the baby turns in its own waiting room,
as restlessly as I now turn
a health-book page in a half-learned language:
Let's guard against (illegible);
be sure to (illegible) *every day!*

But here's the man who can read it all:
the doctor – handsome, young, a bit proud,
as if the father of all our children –
billows in on a white, open-coated sail
and, bowing to us with nautical
briskness, takes the time to wish
the mates a benevolent good morning.

We murmur in kind; then, in a hush,
some dozen heads in unison
swivel to follow his form until
it vanishes behind a door.
Daily, I think, women just like us
are found normal there. Who shall be the first?
It's Mrs. Hino – although the nurse

has to call her twice, across the length
of eight abstracted months. She rises
slowly, resting, in a universal
gesture I've only begun to read,
one hand on the swell below her breasts
as though what's borne within
were here, and could be taken in her arms.

Al Young

FOR ARL IN HER SIXTH MONTH

Cool beneath melon–colored cloth, your belly –
a joyous ripening that happens & happens,
that gently takes root & takes over,
a miracle uncelebrated under an autumn dress
that curves & falls slowly to your ankles

As you busy yourself with backyard gardening,
humming, contained, I think of your tongue
at peace in its place; another kind of fruit,
mysterious flower behind two lips that open
for air & for exits & entrances.

                                  Perhaps if I placed
my hungry ear up next to a cantaloupe or coconut
(for hours at a time & often enough),
I'd hear a fluttering or maybe a music almost like
the story I've heard with my ear to your belly,
a sea–shell history of evolution personified

Your womb is a room where it's always afternoon

Mary Balazs

PREGNANT TEENAGER ON THE BEACH

From her pool in the muddy shallows
she squints sixty yards out
at the white blister of the sunning deck.
On the diving board
a girl her own age shrieks,
topples with a bronzed youth
into the green water.
Separately they rise, an arc of light
like a rapier between them.
Laughing,
their glances fence,

lock.

Before her, in water low as their knees,
a circle of mothers
tow children on inflated plastic ducks,
sprinkle the murky water
over their sun-burned thighs.
She looks into their eyes:
can they remember a night
when the stars rose like a host
in the spring sky?

She stares at her abdomen
where beneath the tight skin
a sea churns,
alive with that small fish
whose gills prepare for the barbed air.
A heavy wave pulls her to shore,
drops her among stones

and cracked shells.

Barbara Ras

PREGNANT POETS SWIM LAKE TARLETON, NEW HAMPSHIRE

For Emily Wheeler

You dive in, head for the other side, sure
that to swim a lake means to cross it,
whole. I am slow to follow,
repelled by edgewater rife with growth, the darker
suck of the deep. You lead,
letting go so surely you possess. I surrender.
Midlake we rest, breathless, let up our feet.
Our bellies are eight-month fruits
fabulous with weightlessness.
We have entered summer like a state of pasture,
pregnancy like a state of mind so full
nothing else can be.
Sharing this is simple: the surprise of a tomato
still perfect after days in a pocket.
Brown lines began in pubic hair, arced
up abdomens to our navels.
Here is the circle made flesh.
How much water does it take to make blood?
Where do Tibetans get the conches
they blow to release the trapped sound of the sea?
Our talk slows to the lengthening loop of the blood,
pauses for tiny hands, tiny feet to beat their sayso.
'Marianne' lasts as long as a complete sentence
before the next utterance floats up, Moore.'
We are the gardens. We are the toads.
The season of wetness is upon us.
Leap. Leap for all the kingdoms
and all the waters,
the water that breaks,
the rain, the juice, the tide,
the dark water that draws light down to life.

Robert Lowell

NINTH MONTH

For weeks, now months, the year in burden goes,
a happiness so slow burning, it is lasting;
our animated nettles are black slash
by August. Today I leaned through lunch on my elbows,
watching my nose bleed red lacquer on the grass;
I see, smell and taste blood in everything –
I almost imagine your experience mine.
This year by miracle, you've jumped from 38
to 40, joined your elders who can judge:
woman has never forgiven man her blood.
Sometimes the indictment dies in your forgetting.
You move on crutches into your ninth month,
you break things now almost globular –
love in your fullness of flesh and heart and humor.

Emily Grosholz

THIRTY-SIX WEEKS

Ringed like a tree or planet, I've begun
to feel encompassing,
and so must seem to my inhabitant
who wakes and sleeps in me, and has his being
who'd like to go out walking after supper
although he never leaves the dining room,
timid, insouciant, dancing on the ceiling.

I'm his roof, his walls, his musty cellar
lined with untapped bottles of blue wine.
His beach, his seashell combers
tuned to the minor tides of my placenta,
wound in the single chamber of my whorl.
His park, a veiny meadow
plumped and watered for his ruminations,

a friendly climate, sun and rain combined
in one warm season underneath my heart.

Beyond my infinite dark sphere of flesh
and fluid, he can hear two voices talking:
his mother's alto and his father's tenor
aligned in conversation.
Two distant voices, singing beyond the pillars
of his archaic Mediterranean,
reminding him to dream
the emerald outness of a brave new world.

Sail, little craft, at your appointed hour,
your head the prow, your lungs the sails
and engine, belly the seaworthy nave,
and see me face to face:
No world, no palace, no Egyptian goddess
started over heaven's poles,
only your pale, impatient, opened mother
reaching to touch you after the long wait.

Only one of two, beside your father,
speaking a language soon to be your own.
And strangely, brightly clouding out behind us,
at last you'll recognize
the greater earth you used to take me for,
ocean of air and orbit of the skies.

Kathleen Fraser

POEMS FOR THE NEW

1.

we're connecting,
    foot under my rib.
I'm sore with life!
At night,

    your toes grow. Inches of the new!
The lion prowls the sky
and shakes his tail for you.
Pieces of moon
    fly by my kitchen window.
And your father comes
riding the lions back
    in the dark,
to hold me,
    you,
        in the perfect circle of him.

2.

Voluptuous against him, I am
nothing superfluous,
but all —
bones, bark of him, root of him take.
I am round
with his sprouting,
new thing new thing!
He wraps me.
The sheets are white.
My belly has tracks on it —
                hands and feet
are moving
under this taut skin.
In snow, in light,
we are about to become!

Anne Halley

O DOCTOR DEAR MY LOVE

O doctor dear my love, admit
there are enough. Why should we need
justifiable worldwide fear,
whether the sneaky drug deforming
quietly, from inside out, or
the drizzle, firestorming doom
out there, invisible, swarming –
no scabrous ooze, secretive sore
and not the loosehung head
of what I saw led down the road,
an emptiness, a waste in bulging skin.
But this. Enough has not enough.

   Dear ministrant, dear doctor
exhume this blade of flesh with your bright steel.
Come succor me, believable monsters.

On the other side, no easy matter.
Think on the others, love, my doctor:
think the milked male, the humiliating
dash across a dawnwhite street,
the locked laboratory,
but the semen caught, deliverable,
hot from the press; think latex lady
inside whose whorly layers nothing takes.
Think those slitherings, bedpans, trickles,
salt tears to float fishes
smell on only –
Think so much hard, some human, work.

Enough and not enough makes less.
Monsters we suffer as we will,
Old Sawbones, sorcerer, we waste
in rubber skins, in little death:

   O dear my doctor, love, be still
Hush, surgeon, little friend, come fast.

Helen Hoffman

NIGHT JOURNEY

it is a hot wind   the breathing
is strong and heavy
nine months pregnant you scrub
the floor and the back porch
and the steps
there is so much energy
the beans are picked and stored
for tomorrow's supper   and today
the rosebush pushed past
its old mark on the windowsill
this is the last day of summer
what is it the body knows
as it dances across the room
for no reason
a young girl wakes up
from her long coma   asks
for her hairbrush and mirror
two hours later she dies
tonight you go to sleep
the alarm clock set
the body
already turning its face
toward the open road

Sandra McPherson

PREGNANCY

It is the best thing.
I should always like to be pregnant.

Tummy thickening like a yoghurt.
Unbelievable flower.

A queen is always pregnant with her country.
Sheba of questions

Or briny siren
At her difficult passage,

One is the mountain that moves
Toward the earliest gods.

Who started this?
An axis, a quake, a perimeter.

I have no decisions to master
That could change my frame

Or honor.
Immaculate. Or if it was not, perfect.

Pregnant, I'm highly explosive –
You can feel it, long before

Your seed will run back to hug you –
Squaring and cubing

Into reckless bones, bouncing odd ways
Like a football.

The heart sloshes through the microphone
Like falls in a box canyon.

The queen's only a figurehead.
Nine months pulled by nine

Planets, the moon slooping
Through its amnion sea.

Trapped, stone-mad...and three
Beings' lives gel in my womb.

Margo Magid

NIGHT WATCH

For Jean

inside   the child
is motionless, or moves
by day, paces
almost human
at night drums
its tattoo softer
than moths'
wings beating
against a thin wall
or turns its eyes
inward, two smudges
cannot see, except
by your own sight
or waits
in perfect patience
webbed limbs coiled
in mollusk folds
as if asleep, or listening
or in prayer

seen, it can be loved
unseen, a lodestone,
a sentinel moving
in dark circles
a glimpsed shadow
tracing ancient maps
that lap like tidepools
the walls of its cave

Lisel Mueller

NINE MONTHS MAKING

Nine months making
the pulse and tissue of love
work knowledge upon us;
the hard squeeze against bone
makes radical trial
of love's primal claim:
here in the body truth grows palpable.

Long comprehended, never
till now understood, the ancient analogy
of sap in the root as impulse
toward flowering, as drive and push
toward all possibility,
is proven upon us. Mind
tried and failed; it is body
secretes the slow-spun pearl
we say is knowledge, oystered
in our infinitely expanding
one-man and one-woman world.

Knowledge of act, not cause.
Love's wine has been our blood
for years; we shall not know
what word or weather thickened
the familiar flux, quickened
old essence into separateness of flesh.
Change and astonishment
witnessed upon my body and your eyes
these long fall evenings
unhand the shape, not mystery, of love.

Nor need we know
more than these sweetly growing pains
which are enough to publish
love's increasing refusal
to lie with the biblical dust of our bones.

Linda Nemec Foster

FAMILY POSE

This is my mother and father
standing close together,
one year into their marriage;
she hides behind him,
her face over his shoulder.
And I am hiding inside my mother
making her large, her body so big
that it has become a chore.
She is embarrassed.

But both of them are laughing,
as if someone told a joke.
And I am laughing too,
small and sunken
deep in my mother. My invisible
teeth hold the grin for the camera,
hold the grin tight.
You can see it in the negative:
there, the small white light
that lives alone, that lives between
the shadows of its dark parents.

Audre Lorde

NOW THAT I AM FOREVER WITH CHILD

How the days went
while you were blooming within me
I remember, each upon each
The swelling changed planes of my body
and how you first fluttered, then jumped
and I thought it was my heart.

How the days wound down
and the turning of winter
I recall, with you growing heavy
against the wind. I thought
now her hands are formed, and her hair
has started to curl
now her teeth are done
now she sneezes.
Then the seed opened.
I bore you one morning just before spring
My head rang like a fiery piston
my legs were towers between which
A new world was passing.

From then
I can only distinguish
one thread within running hours
You...flowing through selves
toward you.

Miriam Pederson

ACCLIMATION

1. Water

She carries a fish bowl
wherever she goes.
She is the only one
who sees the fish inside.

She dreams in a shallow boat,
wakes to the swirl
and splash of water,
the leaping fish.

Her hands spread like starfish.
The sun rises
through the prism she holds.
This is the day the fish leaps from the bowl.

She thinks of places
to hide her young one –
in watery caves,
in skulls of men buried at sea.

2. Earth

She prepares tea
against the day,
camomile for heartsickness,
rose hips for aging.

She drives the car to work
wishing it would float
and find a current strong enough
to take her back.

She holds a chambered shell
to her daughter's ear and knows
she too will bite the hook
knowing full well what it is.

She finds the heel
from her child's shoe
on the porch,
a footstep in such a hurry to go.

Judith Hemschemeyer

THE SLAUGHTER OF THE INNOCENTS

'...Little did the clumsy customs official know that he was pawing
through the luggage of the Lone Wolf, a man who had searched
an entire house in the dark for an object the size of a pea – and
found it.'

Recollection from *The Lone Wolf*, one of our books

What was he looking for? a pearl?
and did he find it in the button drawer
of the old, foot-pedal Singer?

Up to the wrist,
he lets three pounds of buttons
slide through his fluttering fingertips,

finds what he was looking for,
turns to go...
Lone Wolf, wait!

See the silver scissors gleaming there?
That summer Mother found out
she was pregnant once more

she grabbed them and hacked
her sweaty gray hair
straight off across the back.

No more church, no store.
She just prowled from stove to wash machine
to line

in that one square-necked, dark gray, home-made cotton dress
she wore
and wore,

stood ironing for hours at a stretch,
then made us look at, made us touch
the veins on the back of her leg,

hot black baroque slugs of blood.
Lone Wolf, try the house next door.
There are no jewels hidden here.

Lone Wolf, you still there? Listen then.
After three days of labor,
the baby finally came

and the first time I saw him
– she was in the rocking chair
surrounded by the others, nursing him –

I burst into tears.
She hadn't strangled him!
Bethlehem.

Bobi Jones

PORTRAIT OF A PREGNANT WOMAN

Today she parades her shape like swellings of song,
The wings that free her, her throne, her tower.
She bursts the land with her being, her brand, her blossom,
Her passion's lofty monument, her belly's dance.

The trickling that was a stream to her hope breaks through its banks,
Swirling in floods. Come, everyone, out of the way.
Where's the great mountain that will not be drowned?
What terror! Look at this. There is nothing loftier.

Along the length and breadth of our fields the world makes its way
O everyone, run to the side. She is spacious as time.
Watch out for your toes. She carries the stresses
Of the season's muse, her mite of a chick's hidden thumping.

And upon her face is the smile of the Almighty.
Who? Has anyone seen this fulfilling before?
On her tomorrow's sunny roof her rapture warbles:
It chirps, a live coal, in the twigs of her breast.

Cautious her step lest she trample the eggs of Creation,
Light her heart lest she weigh down the little one.
She walks, like Peter on water, doubtfully joyful,
Till she beaches her glory's pyramid in a dry Canaan.

Gwendolyn Brooks

JESSIE MITCHELL'S MOTHER

Into her mother's bedroom to wash the ballooning body.
'My mother is jelly-hearted and she has a brain of jelly:
Sweet, quiver-soft, irrelevant. Not essential.
Only a habit would cry if she should die.
A pleasant sort of fool without the least iron...
Are you better, mother, do you think it will come today?'
The stretched yellow rag that was Jessie Mitchell's mother
Reviewed her. Young, and so thin, and so straight.
So straight! as if nothing could ever bend her.
But poor men would bend her, and doing things with poor men,
Being much in bed, and babies would bend her over,
And the rest of things in life that were for poor women,
Coming to them grinning and pretty with intent to bend and to kill
Comparisons shattered her heart, ate at her bulwarks:
The shabby and the bright: she, almost hating her daughter,
Crept into an old sly refuge: 'Jessie's black
And her way will be black, and jerkier even than mine.
Mine, in fact, because I was lovely, had flowers
Tucked in the jerks, flowers were here and there...'
She revived for the moment settled and dried-up triumphs,
Forced perfume into old petals, pulled up the droop,
Refueled
Triumphant long-exhaled breaths.
Her exquisite yellow youth...

Seamus Heaney

MOTHER

As I work at the pump, the wind heavy
With spits of rain is fraying
The rope of water I'm pumping.
It pays itself out like air's afterbirth
At each gulp of the plunger.

I am tired of feeding of stock.
Each evening I labour this handle
Half an hour at a time, the cows
Guzzling at bowls in the byre.
Before I have topped up the level
They lower it down.

They've trailed in again by the readymade gate
He stuck into the fence: a jingling bedhead
Wired up between posts. It's on its last legs.
It does not jingle for joy any more.

I am tired of walking about with this plunger
Inside me. God, he plays like a young calf
Gone wild on a rope.
Lying or standing won't settle these capers,
This gulp in my well.

O when I am a gate for myself
Let such wind fray my waters
As scarfs my skirt through my thighs,
Stuffs air down my throat.

Barry Dempster

MOTHER

All the trees were made
of rings, their light yellow
apples like coins in the sun.
she sat in the kitchen, facing
the fall window, eyes up in the
trees, thinking them full of
planets bobbing in the blue air.
She put one of her palms over
her eyes, then laid it curved
on her belly. Inside, the birth
sac was globed with gold.

When I was born, in that same
kitchen, the sun had just come
out – mother straining to see
me and her apples at once. I
flowed through the smooth cirque of
a red river, eyes tight as fists.
The world was red. Blood was
darkness. But she held me in her
pale arms, brushing away all the
traces of birth as if they were dust.
She touched me, told me what I'd
soon be able to see, her voice as soft as water.

Apple trees are such unadvertised things.
Not many people imagine planets strung
to their branches like some brown and
gold galaxy. Not even I can keep it
up. We buried her by a river where the
water streamlines the shore like a silver
pencil. There's an orchard over the hill.
If she looks up, flicking the dirt off
her eyelashes, she can see the top branches,
the apples kindling the day – golden
babes dropping quietly to the ground.

Myra Sklarew

POEM OF THE MOTHER

The heart goes out ahead
scouting for him
while I stay at home
keeping the fire,
holding the house down
around myself
like a skirt from the high wind.

The boy does not know
how my eye strains to make out
his small animal shape
swimming hard across the future,
nor that I have strengthened myself
like the wood side of this house
for his benefit.

I stay still
so he can rail against me.
I stay at the fixed center of things
like a jar on its shelf
or the clock on the mantel,
so when his time comes
he can leave me.

Alfonsina Storni

WORDS TO MY MOTHER

I don't ask you to tell me the great truths,
Because you wouldn't tell me; I only ask
If, when you carried me in your belly, strolling through
Dark patios in bloom, the moon was a witness.

And if, when I slept listening
In your breast with its Latin passions,
A hoarse and singing sea lulled you to sleep nights
And if you watched in the gold dusk, the sea birds plunge.

For my soul is all fantasy, a voyager,
And it is wrapped in a cloud of dancing folly
When the new Moon ascends the dark blue sky.

And, lulled by a clear song of sailors, it likes –
If the sea unlocks its strong perfumes –
To watch the great birds that pass without destination.

Translated from the Spanish by Marion Hodapp and Mary Crow

Kathryn Stripling Byer

LULLABYE

Snow is lying on my roof.
I cannot breathe.
Two tons of snow lie on my roof

heavy as the sea,
the loft of grain,
the desert as it gathers sand,
and I have only two small flames
beside my bed. I hear the sea

when I lie down, the sea
inside my head.
The candles sputter when the wind blows.
Snow falls from the trees

like sacks of grain.
No seed can root in snow.

It cannot breathe.
My roof is like an unplowed field.

Who walks upon it?
Rafters creak
as if a wish-bone cracked
and I had wished the sky to fall.

James Merrill

A TIMEPIECE

Of a pendulum's mildness, with her feet up
My sister lay expecting her third child.
Over the hammock's crescent spilled
Her flushed face, grazing clover and buttercup.

Her legs were troubling her, a vein had burst.
Even so, among partial fullnesses she lay
Of pecked damson, of daughters at play
Who in the shadow of the house rehearsed

Her gait, her gesture, unnatural to them,
But they would master it soon enough, grown tall
Trusting that out of themselves came all
That full grace, while she out of whom these came

Shall have thrust fullness from her, like a death.
Already, seeing the little girls listless
She righted herself in a new awkwardness.
It was not *her* life she was heavy with.

Let us each have some milk, my sister smiled
Meaning to muffle with the taste
Of unbuilt bone a striking in her breast,
For soon by what it tells the clock is stilled.

Adrienne Rich

THE MIRROR IN WHICH TWO ARE SEEN AS ONE

1.

She is the one you call sister.
Her simplest act has glamor,
as when she scales a fish the knife
flashes in her long fingers
no motion wasted or when
rapidly talking of love
she steel-wool burnishes
the battered kettle

Love-apples cramp you sideways
with sudden emptiness
the cereals glutting you, the grains
ripe clusters picked by hand
Love: the refrigerator
with open door
the ripe steaks bleeding
their hearts out in plastic film
the whipped butter, the apricots
the sour leftovers

A crate is waiting in the orchard
for you to fill it
your hands are raw with scraping
the sharp bark, the thorns
of this succulent tree
Pick, pick, pick
this harvest is a failure
the juice runs down your cheekbones
like sweat or tears

2.

She is the one you call sister
you blaze like lightning about the room
flicker around her like fire

dazzle yourself in her wide eyes
listing her unfelt needs
thrusting the tenets of your life
into her hands

She moves through a world of India print
her body dappled
with softness, the paisley swells at her hip
walking the street in her cotton shift
buying fresh figs because you love them
photographing the ghetto because you took her there

Why are you crying dry up your tears
we are sisters
words fail you in the stare of her hunger
you hand her another book
scored by your pencil
you hand her a record
of two flutes in India reciting

3.

Late summer night the insects
fry in the yellowed lightglobe
your skin burns gold in its light
In this mirror, who are you? Dreams of the nunnery
with its discipline, the nursery
with its nurse, the hospital
where all the powerful ones are masked
the graveyard where you sit on the graves
of women who died in childbirth
and women who died at birth

Dreams of your sister's birth
your mother dying in childbirth over and over
not knowing how to stop
bearing you over and over

your mother dead and you unborn
your two hands grasping your head

drawing it down against the blade of life
your nerves the nerves of a midwife
learning her trade

Audre Lorde

FATHER, THE YEAR IS FALLEN

Father, the year is fallen.
Leaves bedeck my careful flesh like stone.
One shard of brilliant summer pierced me
And remains.
By this only, – unregenerate bone
I am not dead, but waiting.
When the last warmth is gone
I shall bear in the snow.

Lionel Basney

AWAITING THE BIRTH

The limp corn mellows, and we slide
neck, chin, eyes,
deeper into August.
The world's heart stops, we are
slow-motioned in the dreaming heat.

But in this season, now,
you come into your own,
and your own
comes more and more to life
inside your patient heaviness.
Wonder looms
like a storm in the hills,
but we lose no time in waiting,
nor is it late

as if it did not make our business,
the nations' frenzy,
merely its shell.
When it comes
it is time for it.
And in the fall's
sunlit well,
it will come.

Jeanne Murray Walker

OVERDUE

If your great grandmother could
put her old lips to my stomach,
she'd tell you to be born,
get started. *It won't work*
to hang back, she'd mutter. *Sooner*
or later you have to pick the beans,
paint all the buildings.

She'd whisper this advice if
she weren't far away, on her day bed
where the milky shades are drawn,
surrendering her sight
of the huge daisy in the wallpaper
and the ordinary way
she used to find the bathroom.

The more she gives away,
the less she worries. She has already
forgotten her right hand, mislaid
the farms she sowed and reaped,
the crops she haggled over
in the market like a man
then finally sold, saying

Take your licking early, and get out.
Now she's following her own advice.
She sleeps whole crops away,
time running through her faster
than sand through an hourglass,
her brown legs propped in carpet slippers,
her nose tearing the air in little whistles,

while snowfalls shake
the Minnesota sky inside out,
while all around her Johnsons
and Baumans buy and sell the land.
She's getting out of town
and she hasn't even met you.

You are her last great grandson,
tag end, tardy to take your place.
But you might still meet her,
she might still hold you in her stiffening arms
if you will take your licking early
and get out.

Eddy van Vliet

BIRTH

if something should go wrong
– but this is unlikely –
the deposit on the cradle will be refunded

the expense of printing
'we're proud to announce'
however remains due

when she gasped for breath
with a tongue whiter than my dinner jacket
and her eyes rolled
where an orgasm would never have put them

the number of chromosomes was irrevocably determined

from birth onward
the child's sense of hearing declines

the room is filled with flowers
the first six weeks the child is blind.

Translated from the Dutch by Peter Nijmeijer

Judith Hemschemeyer

THE PETALS OF THE TULIPS

The petals of the tulips
just before they open,

when they're pulling
the last dark purple energy through the stem,

are covered with a whitish veil,
a caul.

I like them best then:

they're me the month before I was born,

the month Mother spent
flat on her back in the hospital.

The way I found out —

once, in round eight of one of our fights
I hissed at her, 'I didn't ask to be born!'

and she threw back her head and howled,
remembering,

'You? You?

Hot as it was that summer
I had to lie there for weeks
hanging on to you.

You? You were begging to be born!'

Anne Stevenson

THE SPIRIT IS TOO BLUNT AN INSTRUMENT

The spirit is too blunt an instrument
to have made this baby.
Nothing so unskillful as human passions
could have managed the intricate
exacting particulars: the tiny
bind bones with their manipulative tendons,
the knee and the knucklebones, the resilient
fine meshings of ganglia and vertebrae
in the chain of the difficult spine.

Observe the distinct eyelashes and sharp crescent
fingernails, the shell-like complexity
of the ear with its firm involutions
concentric in miniature to the minute
ossicles. Imagine the
infinitesimal capillaries, the flawless connections
of the lungs, the invisible neural filaments
through which the completed body
already answers to the brain.

Then name any passion or sentiment
possessed of the simplest accuracy.

No. No desire or affectation could have done
with practice what habit
has done perfectly, indifferently,
through the body's ignorant precision.
It is left to the vagaries of the mind to invent
love and despair and anxiety
and their pain.

Mike Jenkins

THE MOUTH

Up on stilt arms
further than he could climb
he takes care, like a mother
handling her new-born:
dew from lips
the night's dawn,
on a pillow-hoist
further than he could dream.

> The banks are wide
> where milky foam slides down,
> she lets her mind flow
> to the mouth where freshwater
> mingles with brine.

> At the point of bridge and estuary
> the child within, woken from reverie
> as if it had wished to remain, ˙
> not pulled out to sea
> or journeying back to the spring:
> leaping, it takes the element's form,
> its first song raining down
> on arched roadway and guiding valley.

Patricia McCarthy

PREGNANCY AFTER FORTY

More than half an average lifetime
I have waited for you, bleeding uselessly every month,
a womanhood denied. And now I cradle you,
my miracle chance, within me where, for a while
you are safe. Learning to float and dance through worlds
that, within the lure of visual images, inspire
your growth, you seem far more advanced than I.
And keep me in the hope where I keep you.

Desperate for the seven remaining months to pass
without a hitch, I refrain from carrying heavy weights,
cool the water in my bath and, instead of eating,
nourish you with vitamins and minerals untasted before.
I wish on you your father's temperament, his hair
which straightens to silk in the rain; not to be born,
like me, over aware, with hair that bumps in depressions.
But to take things in your stride – as I hope

to take you, reciprocal in virtue. There are books
I could read to tell, in detail, of your development,
tests I could have to rule out handicap
and prove you curled up cosily, not dangling
from a precipice, ready to drop because your fingertips
have had no chance to form. Yet, in a way, I'd rather
not know. And trust in the Nature we are both pushing
to extremes as it pushes us: mother and daughter

or mother and son, linked for as long as wishes dare
the substantial. Do you realise you make me
tired and queasy on seas that give you no qualms –
whitening to break on my surprise Holy Land?
That you must be careful of me lest I lose you
to outer years before they peel off their age inside?
For it is in my youth that you grow, in my youth
that I dare call myself, however temporarily, 'woman'.

3

Birthing

'She's crowning, someone says'

Anon [Papago, North American Indian]

SONG OF A WOMAN IN LABOR

towering rocks
sound
in the evening
with them
I cry

Anon [Ten'a, Alaskan Indian]

THE CHOICE

while she was berrying
she bore that child
laid it on grass
and berried some more
she came back, creeping
she came back, creeping
and sprang forward
screaming
to terrify that child
then she left
she came back, creeping
and did those things again
once twice three times
the fourth time the child
changed it was a bird
flew away

English version by Armand Schemer

Alicia Suskin Ostriker

DREAM

a woman
oliveskinned like an Indian
brownhaired like a European
Crouches over a stool
                              in a green room

    she is in labor, she is giving birth
    comfortable, she rides with this work
    for hours, for days
           for the duration of this
                  dream

Rosemary Dobson

THE BIRTH

A wreath of flowers as cold as snow
Breaks out in bloom upon the night:
That tree is rooted in the dark,
It draws from dew its breath of life,
It feeds on frost, it hangs in air
And like a glittering branch of stars
Receives, gives forth, its breathing light.

Eight times it flowered in the dark,
Eight times my hand reached out to break
That icy wreath to bear away
Its pointed flowers beneath my heart.
Sharp are the pains along the way
Down, down into the depths of night
Where one goes for another's sake.

Once more it flowers, once more I go
In dream at midnight to that tree,
I stretch my hand and break the branch

And hold it to my human heart.
Now, as the petals of a rose
Those flowers unfold and grow to me –
I speak as of a mystery.

Jeanne Murray Walker

HOW LABOR STARTS

I lie under one clean white sheet
beside your father.
We are hardly breathing.
Through the formal window
a northwest wind drifts down,
perhaps from Minnesota,
disordering the curtains,
suggesting things in the dark:
wet docks, lizards, lost shoes,
flotsam of childhood
wafting across the mind,
nothing in particular
but still not nothing.
And then a sound
like the whisper of a boat
pulling in at Hallin's dock.
From a wide lake
where incandescent water folds
over and over itself,
the boat arrives
through the fragrance
of decaying seaweeds,
and in the precise moment
it brushes the wooden pilings
oh, something, something
starts way back in the bloodstream
like the faintest trickle
of pitocin invading

this wide night
and I get up
clutching my cotton bathrobe,
thinking
a stranger must be riding
this small boat.
Tomorrow must be here,
you must be lighting now.
Across the cerebral cortex,
across the deep median sagittal groove,
across the corpus callosum
a contraction
comes.

Michael Dennis Browne

BREECH

We called and called but he did not come.
We stared at each other. So we ran
looking for him, twisting, panting
among the trees, losing sight of each other,
making contact again, even colliding
once, more than once, sweat-stung, salt-smarting,
asking: Did you see? Did you? Was there anything?
It was when we were standing panting in front
of the same thick oak where we began
that we saw him, or saw his feet first,
descending out of the tree where he had been
hiding, saw them sliding soundless backwards,
streaked with blood, the skin creased and cheesy,
slowly, slowly, as the tree bark
yielded them, then his legs, his buttocks,
his little wrinkled back, and at last
the matted, clotted hair, the soaked back
of his head, until, with the tree's last thrust
and the wordless closing over of its bark,

he slid onto the muddy ground and lay there,
lips parted, panting, and we forgave him.

Linda Pastan

NOTES FROM THE DELIVERY ROOM

Strapped down,
victim in an old comic book,
I have been here before,
this place where pain winces
off the walls
like too bright light.
Bear down a doctor says,
foreman to sweating laborer,
but this work, this forcing
of one life from another
is something that I signed for
at a moment when I would have signed anything.
Babies should grow in fields;
common as beets or turnips
they should be picked and held
root end up, soil spilling
from between their toes –
and how much easier it would be later,
returning them to earth.
Bear up...bear down...the audience
grows restive, and I'm a new magician
who can't produce the rabbit
from my swollen hat.
She's crowning, someone says,
but there is no one royal here,
just me, quite barefoot,
greeting my barefoot child.

Sharon Olds

THE MOMENT THE TWO WORLDS MEET

That's the moment I always think of – when the
slick, whole body comes out of me,
when they pull it out, not pull it but steady it
as it pushes forth, not catch it but keep their
hands under it as it pulses out,
they are the first to touch it,
and it shines, it glistens with the thick liquid on it.
That's the moment, while it's sliding, the limbs
compressed close to the body, the arms
bent like a crab's rosy legs, the
thighs closely packed plums in heavy syrup, the
legs folded like the white wings of a chicken –
that is the center of life, that moment when the
juiced bluish sphere of the baby is
sliding between the two worlds,
wet, like sex, it *is* sex,
it is my life opening back and back
as you'd strip the reed from the bud, not strip it but
watch it thrust so it peels itself and the
flower is there, severely folded, and
then it begins to open and dry
but by then the moment is over,
they wipe off the grease and wrap the child in a blanket and
hand it to you entirely in this world.

Beth Bentley

THE BIRTHING

But she had seen the cattle drop their young,
their matted hairy flanks soaked with sweat
bony legs shaking. Their milky eyes sought hers,
a swirl of color, of dumb question. Into the dung

and the saw of heavy breaths, blind and wet,
the calves somersaulted, head over heels,
skinny arms and legs crumpled together.
They lay against the cows' warm, trembling sides.
What had that ferment to do with her,
so secret, so alone, a separate creature?
Her small belly fattened, the breasts he had taught her were beautiful
swelled like melons, the nipples darkened. A turmoil
churned inside her, sharp and hard, a sack
of quarreling pullets, something all bone and beak.

Something of her, but alien. The first pain
rippled across her like a caress, so fleetingly
it fell. From her ankles a blush rose and branched
to all parts of her body. She panted, splashing
cold water onto her face from a stream. Crouched
in the shade of a bush she felt the waves begin.
She breathed with them. Once, under her feet,
the earth had billowed that way, rumbled, shifted,
then rent, dislodging the trees. Her nails bit the cheeks
of her palms. What was this uprooting, this quake?
Her limbs flew from her center, suddenly struck
in a black cataclysm, a flick that cleft
her two parts. She fell, fell into the wound.
It was this she had waited for, His transfixing hand!

Shelly Wagner

BIRTH OF A CHILD

The birth began with a silent splash,
my womb weeping.
The crown of the baby's head
opened my body
like a camera lens
photographing the end of our union.
A doctor's hands

as large as the child's torso
freed the right shoulder,
then the left,
allowing the wet, slippery little boy
to burst forth.
He was laid like a gift on my breast.
Our hearts' duet continued.
My heart would not stop
pumping our blood
through the thick blue braid of veins,
my pulse pounding like a fist
to protest the sterile scissors
cutting our connection.

John Stone

TO A 14 YEAR OLD GIRL IN LABOR AND DELIVERY

I cannot say it to you, Mother. Child.
Nowhere now is there a trace of the guile
that brought you here. Near the end of exile

I hold you prisoner, jailer, in my cage
with no easy remedy for your rage
against him and the child. You coming of age

is a time of first things: a slipping of latches;
of parallels like fire and the smell of matches.
The salmon swims upstream. The egg hatches.

Helen Chasin

THE RECOVERY ROOM: LYING-IN

Diapered in hospital linen,
my public seam stitched back into secrets,
I itch and heal in my crib, wrapped
in scopolamine. My lips like asbestos,
I can't make it
out of the medicine. Something has happened:
my belly has gone
flaccid, ersatz as sponge. Screwed
on this centripetal ache, I fix on pain
and breathe it like an element.
My neighbor-women are bad-mouthing the mothers-
in-law whose sons brought them to this.
We've been had. Joyful and dopey
we roll in our girlish paranoias.
The nurses want to sleep with the doctor; they wait
for my blood pressure to go down.
I try to climb, the walls shrug me off.
In my unique visiting hour I am visited
with guests witty beyond belief; before I can answer
the drug subsides, those pretend bastards are gone.
Back in my skull, out of love with the obstetrician,
I read my tag to prove I'm sensible.
The orderly wheels me upstairs to meet my daughter.
Funnyface, sweet heart,
this ordeal has almost nothing to do with love.

Catherine Brewton

MADONNA

The moon keeps watch
outside her window.
When it's time,
she lays her body

on a bed of coats and towels
nested on the bathroom floor
beside the radiator,
taking careful inventory
of the bowl of water
she's prepared,
the scissors, sponge,
she curls up underneath
a surplus blanket, ready,
listening for the thunder
in her belly to return.
The muscles spasm
in the pain
her throat expels,
she tries to focus
on the clothes shed
in a pile by the door,
then on the cockroach
boring through
the peeling layers
to the green wall underneath
that she remembers,
when her hands clench
in response,
her nostrils flare
until the lungs
that overtake her
leave her breathing
on her own again,
her head soothed
in the pocket of an arm,
she counts the intervals
the ticking of the faucet
leaves, too quick and silent
for relief, and welcomes in
another wave to take her
through transition.
Her eyes fix on the window
where the sun breaks

through the bars,
her fingers scour tiles
for the scissors, sponge,
the bowl of water,
for what's hers,
a son
couched in the thick white soles
of her feet.

Charlotte Otten

DECEMBER HATCH

December world offering
only bitter snow
asphalt tinged, a sycamore tree

blotched by its own peeling skin,
sparrows quarreling over
squirrel-spilled seed

my own seed struggling to remain
alive, I toxemic, seven days overdue
tubed, fluids dripping

in my arm, hoping to dilute poisons
menacing my bloodstream,
kidneys,

conditions no earth mother
could have borne, the operating
room blinding me with lights

going under seeing a pure stream
shining with fish surfacing
sucking in a fresh hatch

slipping into unconsciousness

fearing my hatch had drowned
in my polluted stream.

I awoke to water
on my belly, living tears,
together we would walk fresh streams.

Lucille Day

LABOR

All night the Shabbos candles
beat like twin hearts.
I awoke every hour
and when they finally went out
I got up.
It was still dark.

Now, clouds blister the sky –
a terrible rash, all white.
The sun is no poultice,
but the wind
soothes and soothes.

Soon the pain will be over.
I am going to find a room.
It will be all white
except for my blood
and one lamp
burning like a small sun.

I will not notice it.
Cool drafts will cover my body.
Outside the sky will clear.
By noon
someone will be born.

Seamus Heaney

A PILLOWED HEAD

Matutinal. Mother-of-pearl
Summer come early. Slashed carmines
And washed milky blues.

To be first on the road.
Up with the ground-mists and pheasants.
To be older and grateful

That this time you too were half-grateful
The pangs had begun – prepared
And clear-headed, foreknowing

The trauma, entering on it
With full consent of the will.
(The first time, dismayed and arrayed

In your cut-off white cotton gown,
You were more bride than earth-mother
Up on the stirrup-rigged bed,

Who were self-possessed now
To the point of a walk on the pier
Before you checked in.)

And then later on I half-fainted
When the little slapped palpable girl
Was handed to me; but as usual

Came to in two wide-open eyes
That had been dawned into farther
Than ever, and had outseen the last

Of all those mornings of waiting
When your domed brow was one long held silence
And the dawn chorus anything but.

Ann Darr

OBLIQUE BIRTH POEM

Labor Room: three handed
cribbage, interrupted by jack-pot
coming on. Back to the game. I win
three dollars and twenty cents...
Now!
I have never seen a birth before,
hold the mirror over here
and now in her garland of
cheese and while we are still
connected, I am towing you, my little
skiff, my boat, come into my arms,
onto my deck, sunlight has just
shone through, and the crazy doctor
bursts into song. Happy Birthday
he sings in his cracked voice and we
                    are all laughter.

Jon Stallworthy

THE ALMOND TREE

I
All the way to the hospital
the lights were green as peppermints.
Trees of black iron broke into leaf
ahead of me, as if
I were the lucky prince
in an enchanted wood
summoning summer with my whistle,
banishing winter with a nod.

Swung by the road from bend to bend,
I was aware that blood was running
down through the delta of my wrist

and under arches
of bright bone. Centuries,
continents it had crossed;
from an undiscovered beginning
spiralling to an unmapped end.

II
Crossing (at sixty) Magdalen Bridge
Let it be a son, a son, said
the man in the driving mirror,
Let it be a son. The tower
held up its hand: the college
bells shook their blessing on his head.

III
I parked in an almond's
shadow blossom, for the tree
was waving, waving me
upstairs with a child's hands.

IV
Up
the spinal stair
and at the top
along
a bone-white corridor
the blood tide swung
me swung me to a room
whose walls shuddered
with the shuddering womb.
Under the sheet
wave after wave, wave
after wave beat
on the bone coast, bringing
ashore – whom?
New-
minted, my bright farthing!
Coined by our love, stamped with
our images, how you

enrich us! Both
you make one. Welcome
to your white sheet,
my best poem!

V

At seven-thirty
the visitors' bell
scissored the calm
of the corridors.
The doctor walked with me
to the slicing doors.
His hand upon my arm.
his voice – *I have to tell*
you – set another bell
beating in my head:
your son is a mongol
the doctor said.

VI

How easily the word went in –
clean as a bullet
leaving no mark on the skin,
stopping the heart within it.

This was my first death.
The '*I*' ascending on a slow
last thermal breath
studied the man below

as a pilot treading air might
the buckled shell of his plane –
boot, glove, helmet
feeling no pain

from the snapped wires' radiant ends.
Looking down from a thousand feet
I held four walls in the lens
of an eye: wall, window, the street

a torrent of windscreens, my own
car under its almond tree,
and the almond waving me down.
I wrestled against gravity.

but light was melting and the gulf
cracked open. Unfamiliar
the body of my late self
I carried to the car.

VII
The hospital – its heavy freight
lashed down ship-shape ward over ward –
steamed into night with some on board
soon to be lost if the desperate

charts were known. Others would come
altered to land or find the land
altered. At their voyage's end
some would be added to, some

diminished. In a numbered cot
my son sailed from me; never to come
ashore into my kingdom
speaking my language. Better not

look that way. The almond tree
was beautiful in labour. Blood-
dark, quickening, bud after bud
split, flower after flower shook free.

On the darkening wind a pale
face floated. Out of reach. Only when
the buds, all the buds, were broken
would the tree be in full sail.

In labour the tree was becoming
itself. I, too, rooted in earth
and ringed by darkness, from the death
of myself saw myself blossoming,

wrenched from the caul of my thirty
years' growing, fathered by my son,
unkindly in a kind season
by love shattered and set free.

Alicia Suskin Ostriker

THE CAMBRIDGE AFTERNOON WAS GRAY

When you were born, the nurse's aide
Wore a gray uniform, and the Evelyn Nursing Home
Was full of Sisters of Mercy starches

To a religious ecstasy
Of tidiness. They brought you, struggling feebly
Inside your cotton blanket, only your eyes

Were looking as if you already knew
What thinking would be like –
Some pinch of thought was making your eyes brim

With diabolic relish, like a child
Who has been hiding crouched down in a closet
Among the woolen overcoats and stacked

Shoeboxes, while the anxious parents
Call *Where are you?* And suddenly the child
Bounces into the room

Pretending innocence ... My hot breast
Was delighted, and ran up to you like a dog
To a younger dog it wants to make friends with,

So the scandalized aide had to pull the gray
Curtains around our bed, making a sound
Of hissing virtue, curtainrings on rod,

While your eyes were saying *Where am I? I'm here!*

Lorna Goodison

BIRTH STONE

The older women wise and tell Anna
first time baby mother,
'hold a stone upon your head and follow
a straight line go home.'
For like how Anna was working in the
field, grassweeder
right up till the appointed hour
that the baby was to come.
Right up till the appointed hour
when her clear heraldic water
broke free and washed her down.
Dry birth for you young mother,
the distance between field and home
come in like the Gobi desert now.
But your first baby must born abed.
Put the woman stone on your head
and walk through no man's land
go home. When you walk, the stone
and not you yet, will bear down.

Sally Harris Sange

EPITHALAMIUM

Molding a steady hand over the brow
and cheek of Noah, my only child, deep
in that other world, I breathe once for him,
then tighten the knot of my coat up over the ripened
belly. Stepping out, it is cold and clear
as stars. The moon still wanes. I see that Gary
holds me alone in his dreaming head as he makes
a place in his car and later, as before,
in bed, laboring, bringing life to the coming
child. 'You're coming down,' he declares, for now

I breathe for him, climbing the serial peaks,
wondering, *who will give this birth?*

The whooshing sound of heartbeat floods our ears
and somewhere, in a cavern lost to us,
a tiny signet ring, simple, without
jewel, expands to accommodate the new
prince. Now Joe tries it on: first
one finger, then another, now three
at once and the longest one that ruins the dam,
draws the secret waters through, anoints
this bed where no one ever sleeps or loves –
or do we? And here a bracelet for me, a token,
an engagement, but who will marry?
Who will give this birth?

I lie back into Gary's expert effleurage.
Joe, fingering my toes, wants to tell me,
'This is our only here: these hands, these feet,
this pull of bone and flesh from bone
and flesh.' 'There's a long plateau,' is Gary's reply
as I try to see far off, below, try
to keep my balance. 'Be with me, Sally.' 'Come on.
Hold your breath.' I want us all to marry
in this chapel. Bright lights, a witness
here and there; someone's coming late.
When lightning glows in the temple – mine – I strain
to find its source. Having been here before, forgo
the white gown and full bouquet, bend down
to see the petals of a single bud
open, glisten, *give this birth*.

Kneeling now at my head, the man who slipped
into the ring the coded message. Again,
I yield to him. We try to receive one another,
flatly, breathlessly ask, 'How you doing?'
And Joe: 'What about me?' You are someone
else's father, Joe – someone else's
lover. Who gave you the wordlessness you carry

here? Whose need informs the simplicity
of your hands familiar with need? What calls
you back from this altar of the body, where each
may place his gift according to his place
and not his gift? And so for a long moment
we rearrange ourselves, forget our allegiances,
say only to one another: *give birth*.

Then the lights must be turned low; no one
speaks; we see more darkness pushing through,
gathering its life into ours, flipping
onto the slackness of my belly, creamy
with being life on the other side, a girlchild!
still mine. When she learns she cannot grasp
it with her fingertips, our Kate gasps
at our air. We stop. Joe comes between us and
the blue pulsing ends. And this decides
the moment of our marrying. Bracelets
are exchanged. Joe peeks in
to see what more will come, but this is all.
Nothing more will come of us. *This birth:*
this is all.

Gary believes she looks like me. She doesn't.
She has full, mobile lips and soft lanugo
cheekbones. Gathered into his arms, she
rides with Joe to the door. He kids,
'I'm stealing this one.'
And why not? Even as we're making free, we claim
a certain custody of all the things we hold
in the momentary circles of our arms.

Dorothy Livesay

SERENADE FOR STRINGS

For Peter

I

At nine from behind the door
The tap tapping
Is furtive, insistent:
Recurrent, imperative
The I AM crying
Exhorting, compelling

At eleven louder!
Wilderness shaking
Boulders uprolling
Mountains creating

And deep in the cavern
No longer the hammer
Faintly insistent
No longer the pickaxe
Desperate to save us
But minute by minute
The terrible knocking
God at the threshold!
Knocking down darkness
Battering daylight.

II

O green field
O sun soaked
On lavish emerald
Blade and sharp bud piercing
O green field
Cover and possess me
Shield me in brightness now
From the knocking
The terrible knocking...

III

Again...Again...O again,
Midnight. A new day.
Day of days
Night of nights
Lord of lords.

Good Lord deliver us
Deliver us of the new lord
Too proud for prison
Too urgent for the grave...
Deliver us, deliver us.

> *O God the knocking*
> *The knocking attacking*
> *No breath to fight it*
> *No thought to bridge it*
> *Bare body wracked and writhing*
> *Hammered and hollowed*
> *To airless heaving.*

IV

The clock now. Morning.
Morning come creeping
Scrublady slishing
And sloshing the waxway
And crying O world
Come clean
Clean for the newborn
The sun soon rising...

Rising and soaring
On into high gear...
Sudden knowledge!
Easy speedway
Open country
Hills low-flying
Birds up-brooding
Clouds caressing
A burning noon-day...

Now double wing-beat
Breasting body
Till cloudways open
Heaven trembles:
  And blinding
    searing
      terrifying
        cry!

The final bolt has fallen,
The firmament is riven.

V

Now it is done:
Relax. Release.
And here, behold your
handiwork:
Behold — a man!

Greg Pape

MORNING OF THE FIRST BIRTH

She wakes before dawn
not quite alone in an upstairs room
of a blue house and breathes out
the apprehensions and in the hopes
of that house above the braided channels
of the river moving through the valley
between the abruptly rising
Bitterroot range and the rounded
hilly shapes of the Sapphires.
She feels a dampness beneath her
on the sheets and begins to suppose.

She has come down the stairs
and stands beside the bed
where he lies on his right side

curled in a sleeping bag. Light
from the sun that rose over the Sapphires
an hour ago shines through the east window
and touches his night-tousled hair.
She thinks it's a good sign. No storm
today. No black ice on the roads.
She stands a moment more, looking at him,
feeling a globe lightness turning
planet heavy. Then she wakes him,
and tells him it's time.

He stands until steam rises
then steps into the rush of water
that wakes his skin. He thinks of a song,
'Many Rivers to Cross,' but doesn't sing.
He reaches for the soap and washes
quickly as his mind begins to race
with the things he must do because today
is the day.

She is talking on the phone to someone
at the hospital twenty miles north.
She is saying yes to questions
and someone is saying yes to her.

They walk out together into the day,
this man and this woman with a child
stirring in her body, carrying the weight
and promise of all the days
since the day they first beheld each other
in a parking lot in San Antonio.

They look at each other differently now,
and the question they don't ask
is there before them. The answer is yes.
Yes is the word, made with so little breath,
indrawn or expelled. Yes, smallest of winds
that set a life in motion,
on which a life depends.

Carol Shields

THE NEW MOTHERS

Nearly seven,
walls loosen, it's already dark,
dinner trays rattle by,
nurses slack off, catch
a smoke, let go.
Roses bloom in every room.

Nearby
the egg-bald babies lie, stretching
pink like rows of knitting,
insects in cases, and cry
tiny metal tunes,
hairpins scratching
sky.

The mothers gather
together in clutches
of happy nylon,
brushing and brushing their hair.

They bunch at the frosted windows
in quilted trios
watching the parking lot where

pair after pair
the yellow headlights are
through blowing snow —
the fathers
            are coming

Helen Sorrells

TO A CHILD BORN IN TIME OF SMALL WAR

Child, you were conceived in my upstairs room,
my girlhood all around. Later I spent
nights there alone imploring the traitor moon
to keep me childless still. I never meant
to bear you in this year of discontent.

Yet you were there in your appointed place,
remnant of leaving, of a sacrament.
Child, if I loved you then, it was to trace
on a cold sheet your likeness to his absent face.

In May we were still alone. That month your life
stirred in my dark, as if my body's core
grew quick with wings. I turned away, more wife
than mother still, unwilling to explore
the fact of you. There was an orient shore,
a tide of hurt, that held my heart and mind.
It was as if you lived behind a door
I was afraid to open, lest you bind
my breaking. Lost in loss, I was not yours to find.

I swelled with summer. You were hard and strong,
making me know you were there. When the mail
brought me no letter, and the time was long
between the war's slow gains, and love seemed frail,
I fought you. You were error, judgment, jail.
Without you, there were ways, I, too, could fight
a war. Trapped in your growing, I would rail
against your grotesque carriage, swollen, tight.
I would have left you, and I did in dreams of flight.

Discipline of the seasons brought me round.
Earth comes to term and so, in time, did we.
You are a living thing of sight and sound.
Nothing of you is his, you are all of me:
your sex, gray eye, the struggle to be free
that made your birth like death, but I awake

for that caught air, your cry. I try to see,
but cannot, the same lift his eyebrows take.
Child, if I love you now, it's for your own sake.

Hugh MacDiarmid

LO! A CHILD IS BORN

I thought of a house where the stones seemed suddenly changed
And became instinct with hope, hope as solid as themselves,
And the atmosphere warm with that lovely heat,
The warmth of tenderness and longing souls, the smiling anxiety
That rules a home where a child is about to be born.
The walls were full of ears. All voices were lowered.
Only the mother had the right to groan or complain.
Then I thought of the whole world. Who cares for its travail
And seeks to encompass it in like lovingkindness and peace?
There is a monstrous din of the sterile who contribute nothing
To the great end in view, and the future fumbles,
A bad birth, not like the child in that gracious home
Heard in the quietness turning in its mother's womb,
A strategic mind already, seeking the best way
To present himself to life, and at last, resolved,
Springing into history quivering like a fish,
Dropping into the world like a ripe fruit in due time –
But where is the Past to which Time, smiling through her tears
At her new-born son, can turn crying: 'I love you?'

Thom Gunn

BABY SONG

From the private ease of Mother's womb
I fall into the lighted room.

Why don't they simply put me back
Where it is warm and wet and black?

But one thing follows on another.
Things were different inside Mother.

Padded and jolly I would ride
The perfect comfort of her inside.

They tuck me in a rustling bed
– I lie there, raging, small, and red.

I may sleep soon, I may forget,
But I won't forget that I regret.

A rain of blood poured round her womb,
But all time roars outside this room.

Vassar Miller

ON APPROACHING MY BIRTHDAY

My mother bore me in the heat of summer
when the grass blanched under sun's hammer stroke
and the birds sang off key, panting between notes,
and the pear trees once all winged with whiteness
sagged, breaking with fruit, and only the zinnias,
like harlots, bloomed out vulgar and audacious,
and when the cicadas played all day long
their hidden harpsichords accompanying
her grief, my mother bore me, as I say,
then died shortly thereafter, no doubt
of her disgust and left me her disease
when I grew up to wither into truth.

Jill Dawson

THE CROSSING

All night the sea tossed me
like egg yolk in a basin
and rocked the baby in my belly

So here, arriving,
it is not I, but we
all churned up and frothing
with still, at the window
the sea of our crossing.

Milky, simmering,
she laps at our door
while I'm lying in water,
drowning, distraught

Even in the bath
I'm assailed by kicks
the vicious struggle
of an ugly chick

I lie fearful at night
while wind, rain and sea
puncture the fine membrane of the house

and the child inside
rolls like an eyeball
beneath skin grown fine as an eyelid

Anne Halley

AGAINST DARK'S HARM

The baby at my breast
suckles me to rest.
Who lately rode my blood
finds me further flood,

pulls me to his dim
unimagined dream.

Amulet and charm
against dark's harm,
coiled in my side,
shelter me from fright
and the edged knife,
despair, distress
and all self-sickness.

Sylvia Plath

MORNING SONG

love set you going like a fat gold watch.
the midwife slapped your footsoles, and your bald cry
took its place among the elements.

our voices echo, magnifying your arrival. new statue.
in a drafty museum, your nakedness
shadows our safety. we stand round blankly as walls.

i'm no more your mother
than the cloud that distils a mirror to reflect its own slow
effacement at the wind's hand.

all night your moth-breath
flickers among the flat pink roses. i wake to listen;
a far sea moves in my ear.

one cry, and i stumble from bed. cow-heavy and floral
in my victorian nightgown.
your mouth opens clear as a cat's. the window square

whitens and swallows its dull stars. and now you try
your handful of notes;
the clear vowels rise like balloons.

Vernon Watkins

BEFORE A BIRTH

Hear the finger of God, that has fixed the pole of the heavens.
There the Pleiades spin, and Orion, that great hunter.
Stars silver the night, where Hercules moves with Arcturus.
Spawning systems amaze: they respond to an ordered music.
Ultimate distance vibrates, close to that intimate string.

Stoop, for nothing can weigh the inscrutable movement of beech leaves
Silken, of brightest green, which May has transfigured like music
Born of their trumpet-like buds; this movement, ever so little,
Hangs on a leaf-hidden breath, so near to the nest of the greenfinch;
Nothing so secret as this, under the shadows of Spring.

Love, your measure is full: the stars of infinite distance,
Needing the shade of a bird to knit our time to the timeless,
Fell to-night through the dusk. Ear close to the ground-root, I listened,
Feeling the sunlight fall through May's untranslatable evening;
Then, upon earth, my pulse beat with the pulse of the dead.

Guests go into the house. On the floor, attended by shadows,
Late I can hear one walk, a step, and a fruitful silence.
Touch, finger of Wine, this well of crystalline water
And this earthenware jug, that knows the language of silence;
Touch, for darkness is near, that brings your glory to bed.

Louis MacNeice

PRAYER BEFORE BIRTH

I am not yet born; O hear me.
Let not the bloodsucking bat or the rat or the stoat or the
  club-footed ghoul come near me.

I am not yet born, console me.
I fear that the human race may with tall walls wall me,
  with strong drugs dope me, with wise lies lure me,
    on black racks rack me, in blood-baths roll me.

I am not yet born; provide me
With water to dandle me, grass to grow from me, trees to talk
  to me, sky to sing to me, birds and a white light
    in the back of my mind to guide me.

I am not yet born; forgive me
For the sins that in me the world shall commit, my words
  when they speak me, my thoughts when they think me,
    my treason engendered by traitors beyond me,
      my life when they murder by means of my
        hands, my death when they live me.

I am not yet born; rehearse me
In the parts I must play and the cues I must take when
  old men lecture me, bureaucrats hector me, mountains
    frown at me, lovers laugh at me, the white
      waves call me to folly and the desert calls
        me to doom and the beggar refuses
          my gift and my children curse me.

I am not yet born; O hear me,
Let not the man who is beast or who thinks he is God
  come near me.

I am not yet born; O fill me
With strength against those who would freeze my
  humanity, would dragoon me into a lethal automaton,

would make me a cog in a machine, a thing with
one face, a thing, and against all those
who would dissipate my entirety, would
blow me like thistledown hither and
thither or hither and thither
like water held in the
hands would spill me.

Let them not make me a stone and let them not spill me.
Otherwise kill me.

Constance Urdang

BIRTH

Before, there was one
Without a name

I killed it
It had no heart

One wrenched away
With a single cry

My body floated
Inches above the bed

Another drowned
In freshets of blood

It was warm in the bed
But a cold hand touched my heart

In the eyes of the newborn
I see an ancient woman

She thinks nothing was
Before she came.

Anne Sexton

UNKNOWN GIRL IN THE MATERNITY WARD

Child, the current of your breath is six days long.
You lie, a small knuckle on my white bed;
lie, fisted like a snail, so small and strong
with love. At first hunger is not wrong.
The nurses nod their caps; you are shepherded
down starch halls with the other unnested throng
in wheeling baskets. You tip like a cup; your head
moving to my touch. You sense the way we belong.
But this is an institution bed.
You will not know me very long.

The doctors are enamel. They want to know
the facts. They guess about the man who left me,
some pendulum soul, going the way men go
and leave you full of child. But our case history
stays blank. All I did was let you grow.
Now we are here for all the ward to see.
They thought I was strange, although
I never spoke a word. I burst empty
of you, letting you learn how the air is so.
The doctors chart the riddle they ask of me
and I turn my head away. I do not know.

Yours is the only face I recognize.
Bone at my bone, you drink my answers in.
Six times a day I prize
your need, the animals of your lips, your skin
growing warm and plump. I see your eyes
lifting their tents. They are blue stones, they begin
to outgrow their moss. You blink in surprise
and I wonder what you can see, my funny kin,

as you trouble my silence. I am a shelter of lies.
Should I learn to speak again, or hopeless in
such sanity will I touch some face I recognize?

Down the hall the baskets start back. My arms
fit you like a sleeve, they hold
catkins of your willows, the wild bee farms
of your nerves, each muscle and fold
of your first days. Your old man's face disarms
the nurses. But the doctors return to scold
me. I speak. It is you my silence harms.
I should have known; I should have told
them something to write down. My voice alarms
my throat. 'Name of father – none.' I hold
you and name you bastard in my arms.

And now that's that. There is nothing more
that I can say or lose.
Others have traded life before
and could not speak. I tighten to refuse
your owling eyes, my fragile visitor.
I touch your cheeks, like flowers. You bruise
against me. We unlearn. I am a shore
rocking you off. You break from me. I choose
your only way, my small inheritor
and hand you off, trembling the selves we lose.
Go child, who is my sin and nothing more.

Ann Darr

WAITING

I am through with magic.
This time I will not run the movies
through my head, the bloody plots,
flaming ships, gunshot wounds, boil-
ing oil, burial alive, icicles
through the chest, all to ward off evil.

I can finally let the magic go. Now I know
I am not that powerful.

The hours drag by. The ironing board
squeaks as I bear down
on the striped sleeve of this shirt,
back and forth, back and forth,
flip the shirt to engage the yoke,
steam sizzles out of the iron,
stripes gleam under pressure,
the hours drag, the phone
does not ring.

Shirt after shirt hangs like
a headless chorus. The sheets
stack in smoothed piles on the shelves.
The phone does not ring. What
has gone wrong at the hospital?
No one dies in childbirth anymore.

I am struck with error. Of course
I am that powerful. I should have
muttered out the incantations all witches
learn. I should have buried the bloody cloths,
run three rings around the whiskey bush,
prayed. Now I begin the concentration
meant to save her life. All the strength
I felt when she was born floods through me
floods through to her. I throw my reason
on the floor and glory in the power. The phone
rings. She is safely delivered of a son.

I pick up my reason from where I had thrown it,
drape it around my shoulders, knowing
I will never tell anyone.

4

Male Participation

'Still on my wrist I feel
The reddish fluid
Where the waters breaking fell.'

George Charlton

MORNING SICKNESS

A mother-to-be pukes into the pan.
Out of sympathy I do the same,
Woken from a kind of sleep that leaves you exhausted.
It is that time of morning things are most acute.
It's as if we'd lost our sense of humour.

Robert Pack

EMPATHY

All brains in mammals begin life female; at a certain stage of growth, the
testes of the male begin the secretion of testosterone. If the growing brain
is bathed in this hormone, [it] assumes a characteristic male form...Maturing
male warblers shed their drab fledgling coat of olive green to take on the
bright reds, yellows and blues of territory seekers: they start to sing the
song of their kind.

– Joseph Mortenson, *Whale Songs and Wasp Maps*

Something in me has always known,
my dear, I was a woman once. Though not for long,
only five months (and now,
I must admit, quite dim in memory)
yet surely that accounts for how

I've learned to empathize,
to feel how fertile women feel
awash in hormones other than my own
in tidal cycles of the moon.
I view creation out of living flesh and bone –

not words and not machines,
not art and not philosophy – just life,
ongoing life, as the one goal

prolific Nature cares about...But having shed
        drab olive green, we warblers roll

            our whistlings on the wind
to play the part our searching selves
        are authorized to play.
    Tricked out in yellows, reds, and blues,
testosterone has winged us on our way

            to territories where we sing –
not to compete with your creation, no –
    but to perform (as our male kind)
        songs of embellishment,
songs that indulgent Nature has assigned

    to us for the mere purpose of –
        let's simply call it, *style*,
    by adding color, adding melody to make
        a drab world beautiful,
transforming wooing for survival's sake

(mere replication of one's genes
that force alone might easily achieve)
        to wooing that delights
    in its sweet self, I mean the love
of the *idea* of love. Exploratory flights

            into a woman's mind
embolden me to claim your territory
        as my own. I do not fear
    your whirling heights. My humming wings
can recognize the heady atmosphere

        of your familiar hills,
your open fields, your lakes, since in the womb
        (a parting time ago)
    I've floated there. And yet, my dear,
you must accept my claim on faith, I know,

since women, unlike men,
have not evolved by passing through a stage
in which they must experience
the longings of our sex to learn that barrenness
contains an extra sense.

I empathize enough to know
you can conceive why I might feel a bit
left out. Would you agree,
since it's a girl, to add an 'a,' Roberta, so
we still can name her after me?

David Holbrook

MATERNITY GOWN

The window insulates me from the street,
And you are gone into a cubicle.
The London crowd goes by: the shop worries the girls
Whose fits or stares would suit an undertaker's!
I notice a youth's cruel face in a blue sports car.

The day is warm, the October sunlight strong –
A balm for us, after that wreck of a summer!
Scraps of curled leaves whisk under passing feet,
And as I watch I have Kent cobs to eat.

We have come to Baker Street to buy you a gown:
Why does the soft-lit scene bite at me so?
I smell the foetid tube shelters of war-time
(A news-vendor tied with string): see willow-herb
Stretch purple in the sun, though there are now no bomb-sites.
I weep in a taxi over Waterloo Bridge, just by St. Thomas's
Where our first child was born. I recognise the moment
As when an awareness gels, and I seem to be regarding
Our life from a distant height: 'this is what happened'
Is happening now. I accept that you are pregnant:

The new life walks already where the confused crowds go,
A legacy of isolation bred between us two!
A rag of a queue of boys queueing for a film
Begins to move along, and the arrested scene is broken:
But when I turn, I am changed, as the capacity of middle age
Is filled with a young man's love, in a scalding wave.
I feel the exclusive joy that new lovers feel,
And the need to be, and make, even where annihilation threatens.

Yet as you come back in the smock my loneliness returns:
Remote in your breeding trance, as a woman is,
You seem hardly to know me: so, it's exactly so,
As when you were first big, and you fainted in a queue,
And I stood in wonder, instead of wondering what to do,
Some sixteen years ago, on the floor of a Hampstead shop!
When your eyes first opened then, they looked as they do now:
'Who is this man?' – soft light of creative care – 'Ah, yes, he'll do'
As you saw the love in mine – as you do now, say you do!

Dafydd Rowlands

I WILL SHOW YOU BEAUTY

Come, my son,
    to see the reasons why you were conceived
    to know why you happened.
    I will show you the beauty of the breath breathed into you,
    I will show you the world
    that is a richness of acres between your feet.

Come, my son,
    I will show you the sheep
    that keep the Gwryd tidy with their kisses,
    the cow and her calf in Cefn Llan,
    foxgloves and bluebells
    and honeysuckle on a hedgerow in Rhyd–y–fro;

I will show you how to fashion
a whistle from the twigs of the great sycamore-tree
in the incomparable woods of John Bifan,
how to look for nests on the slopes of Barli Bach,
how to swim naked in the river;

I will show you the thick undergrowth
between Ifan's farm and the grey Vicarage,
where the blackberries are legion
and the chestnuts still on the floor;

I will show you the bilberries thick
on the scattered clumps of mountain moss;

I will show you the toad
in the damp dusk,
and the old workings beneath the growing hay;

I will show you the house where Gwenallt was born.

Come, my son,
in your father's hand,
and I will show you the beauty
that lives in your mother's blue eyes.

Linda Nemec Foster

THE MAN DREAMS OF HIS PREGNANT WIFE

Her body left me months ago
to begin its gradual, persistent
journey beyond its boundaries.
And now even the dreams I dream
don't belong to me: mere fragments
forgotten upon waking or nightmares
where she sits waiting. I dream
of her waiting. I dream of her.

How it was when we first loved,
as if the memory of the sea
covered us: the salt taste
thick in our mouths; both
of us rising from the bottom.
Her legs becoming star fish,
angel fish not opening for the sky
or the earth or the water but for
that dark place not yet discovered.
And in that dark place she speaks
my name, takes it from me,
replaces its solid language
with a pale, hollow conch. Nothing
but the soft, invisible tendrils
of her quiet breath. Thin music
that lifts itself from a green reed.
The delicate stalk trembling
between her lips, my lips, and
the lips of the one yet to be named.

Ai

THE EXPECTANT FATHER

The skin of my mouth, chewed raw, tastes good.
I get up, cursing, and find the bottle of Scotch.
My mouth burns as darkness, lifting her skirt,
reveals daylight, a sleek left ankle.
The woman calls. I don't answer.
I imagine myself coming up to my own door,
holding a small reed basket in my arms.
Inside it, there is a child,
with clay tablets instead of hands,
and my name is written on each one.
The woman calls me again and I go to her.
She reaches for me, but I move away.

I frown, pulling back the covers to look at her.
So much going on outside;
the walls could cave in on us any time, any time.
I bring my face down
where the child's head should be and press hard.
I feel pain, she's pulling my hair.
I rise up, finally, and back away from the bed,
while she turns on her side
and drags her legs up to her chest.
I wait for her to cry,
then go into the kitchen.
I fix a Scotch and sit down at the table.
In six months, it is coming, in six months,
and I have no weapon against it.

Peter Redgrove

THE EGGS

The bird with bone on the outside,
The smooth egg. Melt butter over your egg, let
The yolk shine in its clouds!

Once she poured clarified melted butter
On herself, so that she might shine
Like the moon, and remarked how she could turn

Round and round inside her buttered skin, and if
You take a handful of wet clay and press
A pip into it it becomes grapefruit,

But only if the seed awakes to your touch,
Only if you shine to the seed.
The morning after,

Her shine seemed gone, rainbowed off
In crowds of bathroom suds, relaxed

Over the warm and scented waterskin, but at breakfast

She smiled again like last night and the shine returned
To everything. She spread butter
Over her soldiers and dipped the strips

Of toast into hot egg, the shine
Broke out of that sealed egg, I swear it,
Like a radium of the kitchen (I saw

Our child shine before she was born:
In my dream I rubbed the best butter
Over the pregnant dome and as though

It were white paper windowing with the grease
The first thing that I saw was the smile
Of the babe looking out at me,

Her sucking thumb, and then how she
High up in the clear butter of her mother floated).

Gary Soto

ANGEL

Tonight I find the
Calendar with its days
Marked like targets.
It has to do with
The rationed water
Falling from the North
And my woman asleep,
Legs pushed up to her
Veined breasts, heavy
And tilting with child.
She turns to expose
The belly rising

– not pure and rubbed white –
But tangled in TV
And telephone poles
Howling through boredom.
My hands patrolling
From throat to her dark
Spade of kinks, I
Think of that good day
When this child will kick
His joints into place
And the eyes circle
Points of clarity.
Already the fingers bloom
Like candles, the hair
Parts in a warm flow,
And the pocked buttocks
Are globed with fat.
I know this, somehow,
Though it is July,
Weeks before our dark
One slides like water
Into light, his hands
Tightening on air,
Or the cord that links
One life so he should
Turn, beyond knowing,
to what is also his.

R. S. Thomas

THE SON

It was your mother wanted you;
you were already half-formed
when I entered. But can I deny
the hunger, the loneliness bringing me in
from myself? And when you appeared

before me, there was no repentance
for what I had done, as there was shame
in the doing it; compassion only
for that which was too small to be called
human. The unfolding of your hands
was plant-like, your ear was the shell
I thundered in; your cries, when they came,
were those of a blind creature
trodden upon; pain not yet become grief.

Michael Harper

THE BORNING ROOM

I stand in moonlight
in our borning room,
now a room of closets
changed by the owners.
Once only the old
and newborn slept
on this first floor,
this boarded door
closed now to the hearth
of our wood burning.

I look over the large bed
at the shape of my woman;
there is no image
for her, no place
for the spring child.
Her cornered shape dreams
a green robed daughter
warmed in a bent room
close to fireplace oven,
warmed by an apple tree:
the old tried to make it new,
the new old; we will not die here.

Ken Smith

FOX RUNNING

Turning hour after hour
the muscling wheel
rode through you

And he saw you now
he'd think twice...

At last you saw
your own body's shafts
and the driving muscle

between them print out
its track, the child
leapt to their hands

and the wheel rolled
out of you, pushing
the small life from you

Ted Hughes

CHILDBIRTH

When, on the bearing mother, death's
Door opened its furious inch,
Instant of struggling and blood,
The commonplace became so strange

There was no looking at table or chair:
Miracle struck out the brain
Of order and ordinary: bare
Onto the heart the earth dropped then

With whirling quarters, the axle cracked,

Through that miracle-breached bed
All the dead could have got back;
With shriek and heave and spout of blood

The huge-eyed looming horde from
Under the floor of the heart, that run
To the madman's eye-corner came
Deafening towards light, whereon

A child whimpered upon the bed,
Frowning ten-toed ten-fingered birth
Put the skull back about the head
Righted the stagger of the earth.

Peter Dale

THE RITE

For nine months
I watched my speck of love
enlarge and grow enormous
in the great lens of your belly
till your sleep was broken
on the obstacle in your lap.

You wanted me
to watch you giving birth,
you said it was a bond between us
your body labouring.
But I knew my work would take me
two hundred miles away that week.

Unable to help
watching pain cram your loins
I'd stand by
cornered in our cramped room
taking your pulse in the doctor's way

and dear you softly as you choked
for gas, not air.

Your fingers
in their pain clutching my wrist
would gain a hold on me
I could not wrest away in dreams or rows.
The butting head that splits you
bears features I once had.

Initiate of a secret society now
your murmur parturition rites I cannot know,
the breaking of the waters.
And tonight you rest these miles distant;
your time about my wrist.

Jeremy Hooker

BIRTH

I held your mother, child.
She was beyond me.

The shout forced from deep inside
Came shrill: shout
Of a body hurt and labouring
To an end: of a self lost,
Willing unwilled, giving
Delivered.
        I was not afraid
Though a storm's blue light
Flickered on steel, made the room
Tropical, dangerous.
One of the masked attendants,
I held her, beyond myself.

Hair more like seaweed on a stone

Stuck to the crown; then
A creased and slippery form
Came in a gush of blood,
More naked
Than a mussel eased from its shell,
Stranger, more ancient,
Than a creature long-drowned.

Breath came with a cry,
Earthly unearthly cry.
The knot was cut, and tied.

Outside, I watched rain drip
From railings of a balcony,
Form pools on the roof below.

Still on my wrist I feel
The reddish fluid
Where the waters breaking fell.

George Ella Lyon

BIRTH

In the steel room
where one becomes two
we were delivered.
But for a moment
I saw the rope
blue, shiny between us;
then it was cut
tied without pain
being heartbeat and no nerve.

As you wailed in your heated bed
a nurse held the pan so I could see
that valentine we all arrive with,

that red pad of which you were the lily
with the cord lying bleached across it
like a root pulled from the water
like a heartroot torn free.

Anthony Thwaite

AT BIRTH

Come from a distant country,
Bundle of flesh, of blood,
Demanding painful entry,

Expecting little good:
There is no going back
Among those thickets where
Both night and day are black
And blood's the same as air.

Strangely you come to meet us,
Stained, mottled, as if dead:
You bridge the dark hiatus
Through which your body slid
Across a span of muscle,
A breadth my hand can span.
The gorged and brimming vessel
Flows over, and is man.

Dear daughter, as I watched you
Come crumpled from the womb,
And sweating hands had fetched you
Into this world, the room
Opened before your coming
Like water struck from rocks
And echoed with your crying
Your living paradox.

C. K. Stead

'ALL NIGHT IT BULLIED YOU'

All night it bullied you.
When it shook you hard enough
They took you away.
I was shaken too. I walked
The frantic corridor praying
Representing
My terror so minutely
It went unnoticed.

The whole place moaned
As it was meant to.
A door flung out a nurse and a scream.
A doctor in a butcher's apron passed
Tying his gauze.
The nurse returned with forceps.

Your door stayed shut. I smoked.
You might have been dead. Or sleeping.

Bloodshot and drugged you burbled about our boy.
He frothed, mildly confronting whatever it was
Flooded his lungs. I was full of pieties.
We had never been so nearly anonymous.

David Jauss

FOR MY SON, BORN DURING AN ICE STORM

Steven, your birth brought
Such a storm of joy
I had to sit down in the Delivery Room
And hold my head.

That day, even the lilacs
Were borne down
By the diamonds on their backs.

Robert P. Cooke

WHEN YOU WERE BORN

[For Emily]

When you were born the moon was quite ordinary:
There was no wind to disturb the sparrow's nest.
The backyard zinnias spun their gold heads;
The border impatiens sparkled like diamond clusters
at the foot of the cherry tree, no longer in blossom.
That was the morning I returned from the birth room
at five, and walked through the neighborhood
dark with sleep, the morning glories crossing
the garage like lace.

      At the edge, near the garden
I reached out to them as they opened, searching
for all their parts, as if they had been
written for me in braille upon stones.

Now, the same driveway turns into the street,
half-lit, and I think of bringing you home,
each of us listening to Lake Michigan heave
against the shore.

      It was a home-coming
for a simple birth, long wanted and loved for.
I look back through the kitchen window
to where I stood with you in the August grass.
A hundred flowers run along the white fence
to the rose bush, looking as if full of snow
in the moonlight.

      I'll always miss coming home
late at night like this.

John Berryman

HELLO

He*llo* there, Biscuit! You're a better-looking broad
By much than, and your sister's dancing up & down.
'I just gave one mighty Push'
your mother says, and we are all in business.

I thought your mother might powder my knuckles
gript at one point, with wild eyes on my tie
'Don't move!' and then the screams began,
they wheeled her off, and we are all in business.

I wish I knew what business (son) we're in
I can't wait seven weeks to see her grin
I'm not myself, we are all changing here
direction *and* velocity, to accommodate you, dear.

Matt Simpson

HEADING OUT

Did I do that? – stretch their love
to screaming, so that he
could never put her through
that kind of thing again.

Big-headed from the start then? – my
soft skull's flowering judged
neither beautiful nor blessable: a clenched,
a brute fist bearing down; and me

a nine-pound bully-boy who'd learn
waywardness, to breathe their air
peremptorily, to understand head-first –
did I do that? – what love's about.

Mike Jenkins

FOR BETHAN

[1. MOTHER]
He was insensitive then, to the processes
within: he saw the ripeness
of the fruit but not the roots
which reddened its skin.

I felt as though it was always
winter. Doctors tried to prune
my longest fears and nurses
told me to think of spring.

Everywhere the talk of babies
and of children made me feel
old and diseased among branches
which vibrated with birdsong.

Finally, we were shown the fertility
of land below soured soil
and the fissure of light
at the end of our tunnelled anatomies.

Books I'd read (their strata diagrams
denoting pain) soon receded
into the gagging heat
and scalpel-sharp light.

Cord the colour of marble,
still wriggling survival,
wasn't delicate and fleshy
as I'd expected it to be.

She wasn't blood-smeared and wrinkled
but downy-skinned and curly-haired.
I ran my body around her naked crying.
Her arms opened – vulnerable fledgling.

[2. MIDWIFE]
I know the procedure
like a mechanic with deft hands.
Yet, you see, I'm not one
to view patients as machines
with faulty parts.

The metal ear of the machine
lays heavy on her globed womb,
but its digits reassure
as they bleep heartbeats.

Every baby has a different personality:
some grip the forceps
some clutch at my finger.
Husbands, I make at home:
the ward my living-room
as I call them 'Dad', deliberate,
inviting them to join a woman's scene.

Labour. You see why they call it labour.
On her side she moans aloud
sending the whole ward spinning,
as I peer for her body's signal
with my eyes untrustworthy scanners.

I coax her, like encouraging a child
who's learning how to walk:
'Good girl! Push!' I am implanted

in the ground for her foot
to press when each spasm comes.

As sweat bubbles from her forehead
and her legs twitch like two raw nerves,
all I can think of is dinner.
My coaxing turns to threats –
the masked doctor waits
to execute my command 'Forceps!'
My persuasive hands replaced
by his dictating knife.

[3. CHILD]
The pool of placenta
has a trail to it
running in a cord.
I try to make imprints
on the walls with my springy
feet. I hang
like a bat
in the darkness.
The underground streams
all meet
at my heart.

When the time comes
when the pool is almost dry
when she begins
her volcano breath,
when the streams break
on her surface
in numerous springs –
 when the time comes...

My ear remains, tentative
at the opening.
They are shouting at her:
I wonder what
they are building.

I have thrust and twisted
down through passages
just to be a listener
on their drama.

Maybe they are erecting
some kind of monument,
perhaps it is a dam
or a reservoir?
Whatever it is, they pull me
across whole epochs, sluicing
my lungs with their air.
Will I be their currency
or their valuable ore?

[4. FATHER]
I leapt into the strange stillness
and the crystalline light
of the snow-covered hillside.
The streetlamps of the town
were my stars
guiding me homewards.

That evening I wept:
hearing her cries in the guitar's
flight and her heart
in the congas burrowing rhythms.

The labour had gouged
a hollow for your mouth
and cut two slits for your eyes.
yet made your face into the image
of a baby's when wailing.
On your side, grasping me
as if you were drowning,
but with the same firmness or grip
when she clasped my finger
saying 'yes!' to the world.

You gulped the air
of the room in your efforts,
leaving us breathless.
Your sweat flowed
like milk, fountaining upwards.

I thought of the baby suffocating
as the hours contracted
into a narrow passage;
until the doctor, with the notion
of a ritual, cleaved you
and you sacrificed so much blood.

She was perfect to us:
her skull with an egg
of rock hanging from its back,
her jaundiced face a smooth
sand-coloured shell.
You whispered 'There, there!'
My tears washed your blood
from her hair.

David Holbrook

FINGERS IN THE DOOR

For Kate

Careless for an instant I closed my child's fingers in the
　jamb. She

Held her breath, contorted the whole of her being, foetus-
　wise, against the
Burning fact of the pain. And for a moment
I wished myself dispersed in a hundred thousand pieces
Among the dead bright stars. The child's cry broke,

She clung to me, and it crowded in to me how she and I
    were
Light-years from any mutual help or comfort. For her I
    cast seed
Into her mother's womb; cells grew and launched itself as
    a being:
Nothing restores her to my being, or ours, even to the
    mother who within her
Carried and quickened, bore, and sobbed at her separa-
    tion, despite all my envy,
Nothing can restore. She, I, mother, sister, dwell dis-
    persed among dead bright stars:
We are there in our hundred thousand pieces!

Christopher Nye

MANZANARES

That morning Feliciana was born
Old Manzanares,
who had seen his wife
grow faceless
from caring for too many
gifts from heaven,
worked in the orchard
burning last year's weeds.
But when her time came
he scrubbed out the flames
and creaked down the hill
through the chickens and children
into the thick heat,
the straining fly-hum.

That afternoon
while her father
flooded the cracked ground
under the trees,

Feliciana Manzanares
quietly as a button off a coat
departed,
as if unmoved
by hosts of apple blossoms
waiting for her there
beyond the torn screen.

James Kirkup

TO MY CHILDREN UNKNOWN, PRODUCED BY ARTIFICIAL INSEMINATION

To my children unknown:
Space projects,
My galactic explosions –
I do not even know
How many of you there are,
If ever you got off the launching pad.

All I know is,
As a 'donor'
I received acknowledgement of
'The success of the experiment'.
All boys.
Mission completed.

I gave my all.
Under rigid scientific conditions,
In the interests of science I
Was willingly raped:
The exciting suction pump
In a stark laboratory,
Sterile,
Beneath blazing lights,
Masked assistants all eyes.

That laboratory bench
Was the only home I ever made,
My single marriage bed.
A kind of actor, I performed,
Projected my part.
All systems were go.
And come. My role,
The onlie begetter
Of these ensuing
Moppets.

All happiness! Yes –
After the initial mild embarrassment
At making an exhibition of myself
(In front of all those students!)
Despite the public nature of the occasion
And the scientific dispassion
I endured with moody willingness
The blastoff of private pleasure
That sent me to the point of no return
And even beyond,
Back to where I came from,
Into outer space.

My sample deepfrozen, docketed
Even before the almost endless countdown
Of detumescence.
I was advised, clinically speaking,
Not to think of 'her'
As 'the wife', but only as
'The recipient'. The tool
Simply as 'the reproductive mechanism',
My essential juices
'Prime sperm' (Caucasian).

On to the Womb, the Moon!
Countdown to zero! Takeoff!
Rockets away! Man in space!
Into orbit! Gee, what a view!

Back to the Womb, the Moon!
To the Lake of Sleep,
The Marsh of Death,
The Sea of Showers.
The trip one long ejaculation...

★

Why do I never wonder who you are, wives –
You whose great bowl of a thousand wombs
Bled to a stitch in time?
Even before the nuptial night
Our divorce was final. Could I care much less
About the offspring of my loins, sprigs
Of a poet's side-job? I feel your absence
Only as I might feel amputated limbs.

At least I'm spared
            The patter of tiny feet.

★

Get lost,
Scions of my poetry, my poverty.
I was well paid to engender you.
(Non-taxable income from personal assets.)

Better for us never
To know a father. If only
You could never know your mother!

So be nice, be clever.
Adventurers, in setting forth
Have never a thought for your begetter.
But zoom on in that eternity
Promised by your patron, your donor,
By your ever-dying poet
Who remains
Your humble servant.

5

The Sacred Condition

'What sacred pattern, leaping from time's loom,
Breaks, for the opulence of the breast to feed?'

Amir Gilboa

BIRTH

The rain has passed.

And still from the roofs and from the trees
it sings in my ears
and covers my head
with a bluish bridal veil.

Good for you, my God,
the child is caught in your net.
Look, I will bring leaf to leaf
and I will see how leaf covers leaf
and how the drops blend.
And I will call the swallows down
to marriage from my sky.
And all my windows I will adorn
with flower pots.

Good for you, my God,
the child is caught in your net.
I open my eyes –
my earth is all one piece, engraved
with the stalks of flowers,
green.

O my God,
how embraced we have been!

Translated from the Hebrew by Stephen Mitchell

Gabriela Mistral

IMAGE OF THE EARTH

I had never before seen the true image of the Earth. The
Earth looks like a woman with a child in her arms (with
her creatures in her wide arms).

Now I know the maternal feeling of things. The mountain
that looks down at me is a mother, too, and in the afternoons
the mist plays like a child around her shoulders and about
her knees.

Now I remember a cleft in the valley. In its deep bed a
stream went singing, hidden by a tangle of crags and brambles.
I am like that cleft; I feel singing deep within me this little
brook, and I have given it my flesh for a cover of crags and
brambles until it comes up toward the light.

Translated from the Spanish by Langston Hughes

Anon [Seminole, North American Indian]

SONG FOR BRINGING A CHILD INTO THE WORLD

You day-sun, circling around,
You daylight, circling around,
You night-sun, circling around,
You poor body, circling around,
You wrinkled age, circling around,
You spotted gray, circling around,
You wrinkled skin, circling around.

Mary McAnally

OUR MOTHER'S BODY IS THE EARTH

Our mother's body is the earth,
her aura is the air, her spirit
is in the middle, round like an egg,
and she contains all good things in herself,
like a honeycomb.
She squats and the rivers flow;
her breasts are the hills,
her nipples the trees.
Her breath scatters leaves
on the shifting sands of her belly,
and her knees roll out caverns and canyons below.
Her menses make the ocean floor shift,
and tidal waves proclaim her pain.
When we, her children, return to her,
in ash or in dust,
her flesh is scarred with accepting us back,
and her intestines growl at our death.
Mountains erupt with her agony
and pour us back into the sea
to hiss and spume her orgasm.

Judith Minty

LETTERS TO MY DAUGHTERS #15

Winters ago, I cried for babies, wanted to swell
to bursting with the seeds of lovemaking.
I dreamed through cold
of warm-hearted daughters at my breast
and swore, somehow, you would make me whole.
Now gone away, your own breasts
make ready, and I grope
through another thaw in this stranger's woods.
I search the crusted snow for a sign

of ripeness, a need to mark Spring on the equinox,
and find it finally in lowland.
In this bog, full with the odor of skunk cabbage,
I bend to touch the first blooms:
waxen blossom, shy child folded inside.
I take in the heat of growth, the perfect circles
around each flower, and feel the whole earth
pregnant under my boots, under the stubborn snow

Linda Pastan

MOTHER EVE

Of course she never was a child herself,
waking as she did one morning
full grown and perfect,
with only Adam, another innocent,
to love her and instruct.
There was no learning, step by step,
to walk, no bruised elbows or knees –
no small transgressions.
There was only the round, white mound
of the moon rising,
which could neither be suckled
nor leaned against.
And perhaps the serpent spoke
in a woman's voice, mothering.
Oh, who can blame her?

When she held her own child
in her arms, what did she make
of that new animal? Did she love Cain
too little or too much, looking down
at her now flawed body as if her rib,
like Adam's might be gone?
In the litany of naming that continued
for children instead of plants,

no daughter is mentioned.
But generations later there was Rachel,
all mother herself, who knew
that bringing forth a child in pain
is only the start. It is losing them
(and Benjamin so young)
that is the punishment.

Gary Snyder

FOR A FIFTY-YEAR-OLD WOMAN IN STOCKHOLM

Your firm chin
  straight brow
    tilt of the head

Knees up in an easy squat
  your body shows how
You gave birth nine times:
The dent in the bones
    in the back of the pelvis
  mother of us all,
      four thousand years dead.

X, '82, The Backaskog woman, Stockholm Historic Museum

Andrew L. March

THE REVERSAL OF THE ARROW OF TIME

You shall be born back into your mother's womb,
feel her even heart again, hear air
travel the warming intricacies of her lungs;
be tickled by bubbles in her snaky entrails;

jiggle when she chuckles, walk her dreams,
dwell in the most private corners of her mind,
and have no cell that is not equally hers.

You shall grow down, reaching for the golden egg,
the wild fleck of sperm in the silvery darkness.
There will be no breakpoint, no central pain.
You will accept your dispersal gladly, and no tissue
will seem unfriendly to you, or alien.

And meanwhile she herself will be slipping back
home to her mother's body, your grandmother's,
a half smile on her lips, eyelids half down
so that it is impossible to tell
from outside where her attention lies, your attention.
But your grandmothers also are drifting with you both.
And the fathers, too: their embryo eyes
turn inward, elsewhere, taking you with
them, if
it still is reasonable to speak of you.

And during your slow growth back, as you cross into
the last ten thousand years, ten billion, there are not
any sudden changes, even those times
before there is life at all, where beach waves simply
cycle empty sand; only an ever finer
sifting and mingling, so that you are put
gradually beyond reach of words, or thoughts of words,
or any algebra we might try to imagine.

And the years' monotonous numeration doesn't hold
any solid meaning for you, whether then
or now, frontwards or backwards. And the mother of time
reveals herself, from one end to the other
of the rushing universe, her true form stretched.

Vernon Watkins

THE CONCEPTION

First is the vision. Yet, since God decreed
A living witness, prone beneath the groom,
Are not the stars of heaven like this one seed,
And does not Earth revolve within the womb?
What mandrake screamed? What shudder shakes the tomb?
What infant crying out in mortal need?
What sacred pattern, leaping from time's loom,
Breaks, for the opulence of the breast to feed?
Imprisoned life, lie safe in these curled arms.
My eyes have said you are not, yet you are.
O faith here carried, yet appointed far,
Why should you fear this night, the clustered swarms,
Who hide the ordained tranquillity of forms
Locked in the circuit of your ripening star?

Judith Wright

WOMAN TO CHILD

You who were darkness warmed my flesh
where out of darkness rose the seed.
Then all a world I made in me;
all the world you hear and see
hung upon my dreaming blood.

There moved the multitudinous stars,
and coloured birds and fishes moved.
There swarm the sliding continents.
All time lay rolled in me, and sense,
and love that knew not its beloved.

O node and focus of the world;
I hold you deep within that well
you shall escape and not escape –

that mirrors still your sleeping shape;
that nurtures still your crescent cell.

I wither and you break from me;
yet though you dance in living light
I am the earth, I am the root,
I am the stem that fed the fruit,
the link that joins you to the night.

Gillian Clarke

SHEILA NA GIG AT KILPECK

Pain's a cup of honey in the pelvis.
She burns in the long, hot afternoon, stone
among the monstrous nursery faces
circling Kilpeck church. Those things we notice
as we labour distantly revolve
outside her perpetual calendar.
Men in the fields. Loads following the lanes,
strands of yellow hair caught in the hedges.

The afternoon turns round us.
The beat of the heart a great tongue in its bell,
a swell between bone cliffs; restlessness
that sets me walking, that second sight
of shadows crossing cornfields. We share
premonitions, are governed by moons
and novenas, sisters cooling our wrists
in the stump of a Celtic water stoup.

Not lust but long labouring
absorbs her, mother of the ripening
barley that swells and frets at its walls.
Somewhere far away the Severn presses,
alert at flood-tide. And everywhere rhythms
are turning their little gold cogs, caught
in her waterfalling energy.

Anne Ridler

CHRISTMAS AND COMMON BIRTH

Christmas declares the glory of the flesh:
And therefore a European might wish
To celebrate it not in midwinter but in spring,
When physical life is strong,
When the consent to live is forced even on the young,
Juice is in the soil, the leaf, the vein,
Sugar flows to movement in limbs and brain.
Also, before a birth, in nourishing the child,
We turn again to the earth
With unusual longing – to what is rich, wild,
Substantial: scents that have been stored and
               strengthened
In apple lofts, the underwash of woods, and in barns;
Drawn through the lengthened root; pungent in
               cones
(While the fir wood stands waiting; the beech wood
               aspiring,
Each in a different silence), and breaking out in
               spring
With scent sight sound indivisible in song.

Yet if you think again
It is good that Christmas comes at the dark dream of
               the year
That might wish to sleep for ever.
For birth is awaking, birth is effort and pain;
And now at midwinter are the hints, inklings
(Sodden primrose, honeysuckle greening)
That sleep must be broken.
To bear new life or learn to live is an exacting joy:

The whole self must waken; you cannot predict the
          way
It will happen, or master the responses beforehand.
For any birth makes an inconvenient demand;
Like all holy things
It is frequently a nuisance, and its needs never end;
Strange freedom it brings: we should welcome release
From its long merciless rehearsal of peace.

      So Christ comes
At the iron senseless time, comes
To force the glory into frozen veins:
          His warmth wakes
Green life glazed in the pool, wakes
All calm and crystal trance with living pains.

      And each year
In seasonal growth is good – year
That lacking love is a stale story at best;
          By God's birth
All common birth is holy; birth
Is all at Christmas time and wholly blest.

W. D. Snodgrass

HEART'S NEEDLE (6)

Easter has come around
again; the river is rising
    over the thawed ground
and the banksides. When you come you bring
    an egg dyed lavender.
We shout along our bank to hear
our voices returning from the hills to meet us.
    We need the landscape to repeat us.

You lived on this bank first.
While nine months filled your term, we knew
　　how your lungs, immersed
in the womb, miraculously grew
　　their useless folds till
the fierce, cold air rushed in to fill
them out like bushes thick with leaves. You took your hour,
　caught breath, and cried with your full lung power.

　Over the stagnant bight
we see the hungry bank swallow
　　flaunting his free flight
still; we sink in mud to follow
　　the killdeer from the grass
that hides her nest. That March there was
rain; the rivers rose; you could hear killdeers flying
　all night over the mudflats crying.

Wendell Berry

TO MARY

　A child unborn, the coming year
　Grows big within us, dangerous,
　And yet we hunger as we fear
　For its increase: the blunted bud

　To free the leaf to have its day,
　The unborn to be born. The ones
　Who are to come are on their way,
　And though we stand in mortal good

　Among our dead, we turn in doom
　In joy to welcome them, stirred by
　That Ghost who stirs in seed and tomb,
　Who brings the stones to parenthood.

Gillian Clarke

SCYTHING

It is blue May. There is work
to be done. The spring's eye blind
with algae, the stopped water
silent. The garden fills
with nettle and briar.
Dylan drags branches away.
I wade forward with my scythe.

There is stickiness on the blade.
Yolk on my hands. Albumen and blood.
Fragments of shell are baby-bones,
the scythe a scalpel, bloodied and guilty
with crushed feathers, mosses, the cut cords
of the grass. We shout at each other,
each hurting with a separate pain.

From the crown of the hawthorn tree
to the ground the willow warbler
drops. All day in silence she repeats
her question. I too return
to the place holding the pieces,
at first still hot from the knife,
recall how warm birth fluids are.

Steven Lautermilch

FOR MY WIFE

We are being born again,
getting second breath in skin and bone, vein
and artery, that once in grunion milt by sea and riverbed
died to take to air.

Through you I find new sight, see the egg
face to face, know the fish, grasp the tree and vine and
blossoming play the ape, to pay out more, still
more this cord, our life-line, into time, into space.

With such grace you grow awkward, pantomime and trance
the moon and tides in their slow dance around the earth.
And then, delivered and light, how you shine,
how you shine.

Helena Hinn

37 – 38 – 37

37 – 38 – 37
lumbering around, stately
perturbed, outraged eyes react to my mound
as though my protuberance holds the solution
to their feelings on the matter

– some horrified
others alarmed
at this most natural of parabolas

none think it beautiful
none think it

blossoming
swelling
growing into tomorrow

all consider it strange
– a pub joke
an embarrassment

something to stare at
rather than gaze upon

Kim Nam-Jo

MY BABY HAS NO NAME YET

My baby has no name yet;
like a new-born chick or a puppy,
my baby is not named yet.

What numberless texts I examined
at dawn and night and evening over again!
But not one character did I find
which is as lovely as the child.

Starry field of the sky,
or heap of pearls in the depth.
Where can the name be found, how can I?

My baby has no name yet;
like an unnamed bluebird or white flowers
from the farthest land for the first,
I have no name for this baby of ours.

Translated from the Korean by Ko Won

Louise Glück

FOR MY MOTHER

It was better when we were
together in one body.
Thirty years. Screened
through the green glass
of your eye, moonlight
filtered into my bones
as we lay

in the big bed, in the dark,
waiting for my father.
Thirty years. He closed
your eyelids with
two kisses. And then spring
came and withdrew from me
the absolute
knowledge of the unborn,
leaving the brick stoop
where you stand, shading
your eyes, but it is
night, the moon
is stationed in the beech tree,
round and white among
the small tin markers of the stars:
Thirty years. A marsh
grows up around the house.
Schools of spores circulate
behind the shades, drift through
gauze flutterings of vegetation.

Helena Minton

THE WOMB IS RUINS

This is my coliseum
Old bath of the gods
I hear water and dogs
Guarding all the gates
Gladiators doze
side by side like oxen
Archimedes strokes his slabs of gold
His pure commandments
This is the cobweb
Of a universe the spiders
Could spin away

The white stone powder
Bees mistake for pollen
Will not bloom
Still there are flowers here
Come, name them

Donald Justice

TO A TEN MONTHS' CHILD

[For M.M.]

Late arrival, no
One would think of blaming you
For hesitating so.

Who, setting his hand to knock
At a door so strange as this one,
Might not draw back?

Certainly, once admitted,
You will be made to feel
Like one of the invited.

Still, because you come
From so remote a kingdom,
You may feel out of place,

Tongue-tied and shy among
So many strangers, all
Babbling a strange tongue.

Well, that's no disgrace.
So might any person
So recently displaced,

Remembering the ocean,
So calm, so lately crossed.

John Frederick Nims

FOR MY SON

How the greenest of wheat rang gold at his birth!
How oaks hung a pomp in the sky!
When the tiptoeing hospital's pillowy arms
Godsped him in suns of July.

Then dizziest poplars, green-and-white tops,
Spun spinning in strings of the wind.
As that child in his wicker
With two great safeties pinned

Slept twenty-two hours with a Buddha-fine face
(His hands were palm-up like a dancer's).
Or his tragic mask's sudden pink-rubbery woe
Sent us thumbing four books for the answers.

And the grave clouds smiled over,
Smiled, flowing west to east, countering sun;
Fields at their leaving all spurted up green!
Old fences limped by at a run!

O elms, fling up up up corinthian fountains.
Fields, be all swirl and spangle, tangle of mirth:
Soon you will root in his woodbrook eyes more deeply
(O reborn poplars) than in Michigan earth.

6

Miscarriage and Abortion

'There are no coffins for what is not born'

Nancy Willard

FOR YOU, WHO DIDN'T KNOW

At four a.m. I dreamed myself on that beach
where we'll take you after you're born.
I woke in a wave of blood.

Lying in the backseat of a nervous Chevy
I counted the traffic lights, lonely as planets.
Starlings stirred in the robes of Justice

over the Town Hall. Miscarriage of justice,
they sang, while you, my small client
went curling away like smoke under my ribs.

Kick me! I pleaded. Give me a sign
that you're still there!
Train tracks shook our flesh from our bones.

Behind the hospital rose a tree of heaven.
 You can learn something from everything
 a rabbi told his hasidim who did not believe it.

 I didn't believe it, either, O rabbi,
 what did you learn on the train to Belsen?
 That because of one second one can miss everything.

There are rooms on this earth for emergencies.
A sleepy attendant steals my clothes and my name,
and leaves me among the sinks on an altar of fear.
'Your name. Your name. Sign these papers,
authorizing us in our wisdom to save the child.
Sign here for circumcision. Your faith, your faith.'

 O rabbi, what can we learn from the telegraph?
 asked the hasidim, who did not understand.
 And he answered, *That every word is counted and charged.*

'This is called a dobtone,' smiles the doctor.
He greases my belly, stretched like a drum
and plants a microphone there, like a flag.

A thousand thumping rabbits! Savages clapping for joy!
A heart dancing its name, I'm-here, I'm-here!
The cries of fishes, of stars, the tunings of hair!

O rabbi, what can we learn from a telephone?
*My schicksa daughter, your faith, your faith
that what we say here is heard there.*

Ellen Wittlinger

A THING LIKE A BABY

I think way back: it's twenty
years since sixteen
and dreaming of surfboards
I summered with my favorite uncle
and his new wife Jackie
in that wonderland of tropical
houses south of Anaheim.
I'd stay up late, waiting
for Uncle Walt's ancient Mercedes
to come sheltering
into its cul de sac home.
He was my only hero then, a trombonist
in the age of guitars.
Jackie, retired from professional skating,
skinny, smart and twelve
weeks pregnant, did not keep
vigil with me, fell
into their big bed at nine.

She was worried all day that day,
called the doctor, watered all

the patio plants, then dialed again.
At midnight I could have been watching
Johnny Carson, would have at home,
but willed myself to grow up
while my parents weren't there,
switched to 'Swan Lake' on some
irregular channel, the first
ballet I'd ever seen.
                                        Then
Jackie came sailing down the hall in her white
nightgown as if on ice again,
slamming the bathroom door on illusions.
I waited a full five minutes,
child again, afraid to be trusted.
Then knocked. 'I'm all right,' she said.
'I was ready for it.'

We sat together on the bed
like girlfriends as we waited for Walt,
turning the jar around and around
in our hands. She hadn't called anyone.
No one knew but me.
'It's like a fish,' she said and I agreed:
'It doesn't look a thing like a baby.'
She took the jar and put it on the bureau
by the door so the moment Walt
came in, surprised by lights and laughter
past midnight, she could point and say,
'That's Katharine.'

It's been years since I've talked
to my California kin, my champion
standing fast on the wrong side
of Sixties politics.
But when the bleeding began, my first
tangible loss, I thought again
of Jackie, how, unlike me,
she wouldn't cry, but kept
assuring us, 'I was ready for it,'

then went to bed
for the rest of the summer.

For me it is late autumn.
The season and my mood suit each other –
a kind of pas de deux.
When I wake up mornings
I feel as lonely as a child away
from home. I pretend to get up
and then I do get up.
When you make so large a thing as life
you turn your back on death,
but it is only a small human back
and death is standing right behind you.

Anthony Hecht

THE VOW

In the third month, a sudden flow of blood.
The mirth of tabrets ceaseth, and the joy
Also of the harp. The frail image of God
Lay spilled and formless. Neither girl nor
    boy,
But yet blood of my blood, nearly my
    child.
                All that long day
Her pale face turned to the window's mild
                Featureless gray.

And for some nights she whimpered as she
    dreamed
The dead thing spoke, saying: 'Do not
    recall
Pleasure at my conception. I am redeemed
From pain and sorrow. Mourn rather for all
Who breathlessly issue from the bone gates,

The gates of horn,
For truly it is best of all the fates
Not to be born.

'Mother, a child lay gasping for bare breath
On Christmas Eve when Santa Claus had set
Death in the stocking, and the lights of
   death
Flamed in the tree. O, if you can, forget
You were the child, turn to my father's lips
            Against the lime
When his cold hand puts forth its fingertips
            Of jointed time.'

Doctors of Science, what is man that he
Should hope to come to a good end? *The best
Is not to have been born.* And could it be
That Jewish diligence and Irish jest
The consent of flesh and a midwinter storm
            Had reconciled,
Was yet too bold a mixture to inform
            A simple child?

Even as gold is tried, Gentile and Jew.
If that ghost was a girl's, I swear to it:
Your mother shall be far more blessed than you.
And if a boy's, I swear: The flames are lit
That shall refine us; they shall not destroy
            A living hair.
Your younger brothers shall confirm in joy
            This that I swear.

Mark S. McLeod

MOTHER AND SON

The blood came earlier than they had dreamed.
A woman newly made, she married.
Her broken water buoyed her thoughts,
the blood baptized and the water washed.

The blood came earlier than they had dreamed.
One man newly made, he died.
His broken body buoyed her thoughts,
the blood baptized and the water washed.

Amy Olson–Binder

KNITTING

After three months
Of silent stitching
In that private rocking place
What finger let slip
What growing row of cells
Unravelled, loosing life and
Leaving the lap empty?

Richard Jones

THE MISCARRIAGE

The day we lost the baby
and I came home
to find you
drugged, in pain,
the white nightgown
delicately shrouding your body,

I sat in the chair
at the foot of the iron bed
and listened to you cry.
I did not say much
except that it would be all right,
then cradled my arms carefully around you.
What did I know?
As I held you,
I felt I had been caught.
The brief light of our souls –
child too sad to show its face –
shone upon my life, revealing
all the things I'd done
that can and will be used
as evidence against me.

John William Corrington

FOR A WOODSCOLT MISCARRIED

I know the barn where they got you
the night they tricked each other
and themselves.

In that season, the nights are
full of rain, the sky shakes
like a lost child and for an hour
it is cool enough to love.

Out of such cool love you came
to burgeon day by day,
carelessly made and moving darkly
like the land your most distant bending
fathers tilled, crying for Israel,
hoping for Jesus.

Your nearly mother felt trouble in her depths

where an ignorant angel stirred the waters
with his holy staff.
She sat big on the shack's long porch
watching cars dart South for Baton Rouge,
watching fingers of young pine fondle
tumid clouds above the field and shed
where you took place.

Cars throbbed toward the city. The shack
stayed where it was. And stayed
till her time came. And yours.

At the clinic they found something wrong:
her blood, his seed — your own blind weaving
of them both. They said that you were dead.
And it was so.

Some time in the sixth month you gave it up.
Maybe you heard some talk of what there was,
your sun her heart thundering there above
red as the wounds of Jesus.
Who turned and turned amidst a tideless
inward sea as ghosts of her body
taught your spindrift hands to be
and made a tongue for speech and eyes to see.

For you, what?

Somewhere near in the fields your father
turns the land waiting for a first
bold thrust of green out of the earth's
confusion. Maybe relieved, as mute and
unaware as she, he will watch the stalks
and leaves spread out, will bless
the flower and the bole. Will shout and
carry the first opened fruit,
a pale victory, running down the rows
pulling its long staple through his fingers
like a sheaf of dollar bills.

And you who lost nothing that you had,
no trees or blooms or words
rising against Louisiana's sun, will stir,
if ever, in the evening breeze, a trouble
          missed,
a junction passed and never seen
like a field or shack at the edge of sight
down a highway to the Gulf.

could feel the chill dissension in her gut:
her wanting and her fearing and her shame.
And gave it up. Collapsed, began to junk
limbs and fingers,
the tassel of your kind,
the piggish brooding something like a face.
Each cell dissolved, left off its yearning,
its moist prophecies.

In the Felicianas,
there are no coffins for what is not born
but loosed, a stewy discharge almost the
    same
as if the bowels went wrong.
Preachers, fine at birth, adroit at marriage,
inured to burial,
have no rite for those who almost were.
A near thing does not count.
A miss had just as well be fifty miles.

Just as well: no matter what they say
each coming and each leaving is a feast,
a celebration of the sun we squall to see
and weep to leave: a leaping forth,
a going down, each swings its own harsh joy
and the round of its perfection has no
    words.
But for you, what?
Who lay a brief time within
the confines of her deep uneasy space.

Geof Hewitt

EMERGENCY AT 8

Across the street, my aunt has lost
    her baby: for nearly as long
    as I can think back, we've had to be so
Careful with her: no games at all
    for one thing and brush by her
    in tight corners without even touching
That wall of stomach, breakable as some new egg.

But now the sirens have died in my ears
    like adult voices, come and gone
    and taken her: she'll have to stay
Away awhile, getting better
    and forgetting all the work she wasted:
    holding eight months my broken cousin.
My house is quiet at this time. My mother holds the phone.

Paul Petrie

THE LOST CHILD

She was not no one.

She had a given name,
a drawer of knitted things,
matched suits and sweaters,
a crib under the window
where the sun could look.

'Others will come,' they said,
'to take her place.'
            (And they did.)
'Lucky,' they said, 'it happened now
before...'
            (And it was true.)

Nine swelling moons,
like a small Greek goddess,
she ruled my moods,
talking in a morse code
of thumps and kicks.

But born still-born she was bustled
faceless away
to save a mother's
grief.

Foolish to mourn for someone
who was so nearly no one,
and after five long years grieve
still
　　though less and less.

Possibility
is not fact.
What never came to be
never was.

(Though half of the world's mourning
is for what never
was.)

Still, it was an error
not to take that tiny shriveled body
in my arms,
not to touch that thin, clenched face.

A grief without a shape
is imageless.

Like a hidden fish it swims
under the sea, surfacing
at will,
or like a dark moon peers
through the window of any season
or any mood.

A grief without a shape
is endless
It has no grave.

Judith Minty

WOUNDS

She has been bleeding
for ten days in Mexico.
Ashamed to speak of it, she follows
the coastline with him
and covers her wound,
stops it up
like a crack in a seawall.

Smiling, touching his hand, she
pretends there is no sickness
in her belly, in that ocean
where I swam. She walks
the shore with him,
drives through dusty towns
and climbs cathedral steps.

She prays to the child and weeps
for nails in hands and feet.
Today in the kitchen, 'Oh Christ,'
I cut my finger. I bound it
to stop the bleeding
and told my daughter
it was nothing.

In my sleep I am crying. Nightmares
cannot be stopped up.
There is a child
in a boat. The boat
is sinking, slipping

into the water. There is no one
to hear. The water is red.

Emily Grosholz

FAUSSE COUCHE

Without intentions, even
without the fine machinery
of sight, you looked away.
How riddling now our quiet
conversations seem,
that filled so many sunlit
autumn afternoons.
'Are you comfortable, and warm?
Are you there?' I took your silence
as natural affirmation.
'The sky is blue,' I offered,
'the color your blood runs,
apples gold as your small
corporeal mind. The brambles
curve downward like a spine;
the silver willows lean
as we do in the wind.
If you are inches long,
with closed eyes and fingers,
perhaps you touch the edge
of your mother's vision.'
But nobody attended:
only a little wind–egg
forgetting to multiply
despite all my descriptions
of quick cloud shadows
which, vanishing, kindle
the flanks of the low hills,
the violet woods, for eyes

still closed, I thought, for eyes
still deep in the great blindness
that stands before and after
our interval of light.

Suzette Bishop

DOCTORS ARE SOLVING THE MYSTERY OF MISCARRIAGE

I remember every detail   what I was wearing.   Her doctor
couldn't find her baby's heartbeat.   He told her not to worry.
My sister on the phone afterwards.   The flatness of her
voice answering the phone.   She must be wearing one of those
smocks.   It is printed with small daisies.   His inability
to detect sound.

The radiologist couldn't look me in the eye.   There was
no heartbeat.   I kept putting my hands to my stomach.
A procedure following a miscarriage during which the cervix is dilated.

My brother-in-law sped through the night with the flashers on.
The wind is trying to get into the windows.

Maybe it's as deepseated as that   a memory of leaving my
mother to enter something colder.   He told her to forget
what happened.   I could feel that all movement stopped.
Her twin brother was stillborn.   Some closeness with others
was always absent.   A still moth with moons on its wings.

The silence over the phone.   I didn't know how to cross
the silence.   I wanted to fly to her.

There was a Christmas tree ornament for him on the Christmas tree.
His name was on it in silver letters.   Either the fetus
spreads its huge wings, fringed   is completely or partially
expelled   flies up to a frozen tree branch   or the fetus
dies but remains in the uterus   the grey sky fills the
spaces between the fringes of his wings. They press into the sky.

Where the lining of the uterus is scraped. EVACUATION.
EVACUATION.
A very neat house with many waxy tulips. The dampness of the
air like the dampness of the vagina.   According to other experts

she was bleeding internally.   She awoke in the middle of the
night in terrible pain.   There might have been no voice
answering the phone.   You're still young, you can have another.

Considerable progress   demystifying   Enduring six miscarriages
was almost too much to bear.   Empty.   Yesterday, a
violent rainstorm giving us ten inches of rain.   Water boiled
in the stream across the street.   The level of the water rose
twelve inches in five minutes and churned like an animal
unable to fly out of the water breaking loose.

My sister was born during a March blizzard.   The hospital
was understaffed, and only one doctor was on duty to deliver babies.
There were many women in labor.My mother waited with them outside
the delivery room.   The doctor smiled at her as he was
lifting a baby up.   In labor for over a day and unable to see
through the whiteness outside the window.   My mother and sister
were left on a cot in the hallway.   She wasn't able to nurse.

I walked through flood waters.   The siren sounded ghost–like
as it echoed in the underpass and in the raindrops.   I had
become very attached.   I felt as if I were drowning.
The baby was a part of me.   Pregnancy Loss Center.
Another ultrasound.   Her body was mocking her.The first

words I'd never hear.   I came quickly, in two hours. It
was early morning, stilldark.   The end of August on the edge
of seasonal change.   I wasn't planned and the marriage
was deteriorating.   I was no longer self–propelled but propelled
by something else.   Water rushed down the staircase.
The rushing sound and movement of water.   I remember my
mother stopping the car on the side of the street during storms
like this.   Water pounding the car roof.   Running down
the side windows.

Patricia McCarthy

D AND C

Wrapped in towels and plastic bags,
I arrive at the hospital without medication.
Analgesics could not deaden the pain
of loss. My bloodprints on the floor
of the ward lead only one way.

The medics, wielding scrapers, betray
no emotion in their hints that I might
have sought, clinically, your elimination.
I cannot express how much I wanted you.

In a white anonymous gown, I queue
on a stretcher for the theatre, disembodied
enough to share your limbo. The terror
of operations and gas replace grief
with the selfish struggle just to survive.

In concentrating on staying alive,
I am not the woman who expected you.
I joke manically with the stretcher bearers.
And chat to the Indian anaesthetist

who is unaware that you beat in my wrist
while I go to the holy Bagmati river
where she belongs for your reincarnation.
Then watch the child you could have been
skipping about your lighted frame,

chanting 'Tamsin, Tamsin' – your name,
folding death into life and life
into death, beyond taboos. What more
could I have done for you? I had

positive thoughts, even spoke to God
and got your forefathers on your side
with their fighting blood. One in six

ends like this, they state, when I
come round – still joking from the casino

of bad gambles. They do not know
you have become the child who has always lived
in me, and I shall treat you at once
to the privilege of my happy infancy.

The coffin in my dream, of ebony,
makes a case for your violin
beneath my bed. Its resinous bow
plays the song I sang too soon.
Secretly, I sing it now –

living your life while the fates allow.

Harry Stessel

A CHARM AGAINST PREGNANCY

We wait for the
serendipity of blood,
haunted by
white wicker carriages
and cribs, by
babyclothes of
milkshake colors.

Sideways to the mirror
she reads her pouch
for occupancy.
Into her rich
Egyptian court has
a tiny Moses come?
Is my plum
about to have a pit?
Are her tits more

sensitive,
is she tireder, more
queasy in the morning than is usual?

'Why don't you pray to
a Jewish saint?'
No one occurs to me
but Billy Rose.
St. Billy, send us
blood, a testament
to insulation.
Please, God, blood. I
promise to buy only
Trappist jelly.

Please let blood
mark the door to
her womb, that the Angel
of Life may pass by.

Ruth Stone

MY SON

Having lost my leather purse
Stuffed with all those unpaid bills and trading stamps,
I live with two dogs who sleep on my bed.
I have forgotten who owes who;
More, the lamps wabble, the wiring is bad.
True, there were epigrams which cost me five years of my life;
Nail clippers, address books
Crammed with poems and telephone numbers.
The list of contents cannot classify
My hatchet wounds.
Dismembered.
Part of me is gone;
Concrete proof of responsibility,

Identification, driver's license.
Friends say, where are your numbers?
What will you put in your zipper?
Have you searched the ground?
Who is to be informed in case you are drowned?
The essential family has become myself. A son who might have been
Pays the penalty of oblivion. Who is he?
He sleeps in the old pouch; an unfinished poem
Lying along some roadside where exercising frogs
Rest on his mother's leather
And his father is nowhere to be found.

David Galler

THE ABORTION

(Greenwich Village, 1952)

She came in, recommended by a friend;
Tossed off her coat and gloves
And, flashing a toothy smile, waddled to the sink,
And washed her hands where jutted six large rings.

I gave her the two hundred, and she ordered
The wobbly kitchen table pushed
Under the bulb; motioned you on it,
Parted your thighs, and worked a catheter in.

She left, instructing me for three days
To answer neither phone nor bell. I made
The ginger broth she had prescribed. Time stopped.
We seldom spoke. We slumped inside our dreams.

In answer to the code, I let her in.
The coat. The gloves. The rings.
Newspapers on the table this time round.
I couldn't watch after I heard you groan.

Blood on the papers. Blood all over the floor.
Crooning, she sponged you off.
Scrawling instructions half in Spanish, she
Departed, chuckling. The foetus dried on the stove.

You were sleeping heavily when
The friend arrived. She brought Jack Daniels for us
'To celebrate the birth.' She wrapped the foetus –
'It's for my collection' – and, winking, tiptoed out.

Audre Lorde

A WOMAN/DIRGE FOR WASTED CHILDREN

[For Clifford]

Awakening
rumors of the necessity for your death
are spread by persistent screaming flickers
in the morning light
I lie
knowing it is past time for sacrifice
I burn
like the hungry tongue of an ochre fire
like a benediction of fury
pushed before the heel of the hand
of the thunder goddess
parting earth's folds with a searching finger
I yield
one drop of blood
which I know instantly
is lost.

A man has had himself
appointed
legal guardian of fetuses.

Centuries of wasted children
warred and whored and slaughtered
anoint me guardian
for life.

But in the early light
another sacrifice is taken
unchallenged
a small dark shape rolls down
a hilly slope
dragging its trail of wasted blood
upon the ground
I am broken

into clefts of screaming
that sound like the drilling flickers
in treacherous morning air
on murderous sidewalks
I am bent
forever
wiping up blood
that should be
you.

Gwendolyn Brooks

THE MOTHER

Abortions will not let you forget.
You remember the children you got that you did not get,
The damp small pulps with a little or with no hair,
The singers and workers that never handled the air.
You will never neglect or beat
Them, or silence or buy with a sweet.
You will never wind up the sucking-thumb
Or scuttle off ghosts that come.
You will never leave them, controlling your luscious sigh,

Return for a snack of them, with gobbling mother-eye.

I have heard in the voices of the wind the voices of my dim killed
        children.
I have contracted. I have eased
My dim dears at the breasts they could never suck.
I have said, Sweets, if I sinned, if I seized
Your luck
And your lives from your unfinished reach,
If I stole your births and your names,
Your straight baby tears and your games,
Your stilted or lovely loves, your tumults, your marriages, aches,
        and your deaths,
If I poisoned the beginnings of your breaths,
Believe that even in my deliberateness I was not deliberate.
Though why should I whine,
Whine that the crime was other than mine? –
Since anyhow you are dead.
Or rather, or instead,
You were never made.
But that too, I am afraid,
Is faulty: oh, what shall I say, how is the truth to be said?
You were born, you had body, you died.
It is just that you never giggled or planned or cried.

Believe me, I loved you all.
Believe me, I knew you, though faintly, and I loved, I loved you
All.

Mary Gordon

THE UNWANTED

Instead of you, I choose the blood.
Before your splash, that drag,
Rank stuff, but sure.
It is not fired through.
It is not dangerous like you.
Rationing lightning.

I cannot see the seed you are
Tipping my life
To madness or to worse.
Your growth kills mine.
So tinily you eat me all
To shreds.
I draw you out.
Godless, no mother
I have neither breath
Nor spirit to give up.

Mite, maggot, ovum, sperm,
What are you?
My neat trick, my sweet genesis.
Unbearable. Unborn.

Ai

ABORTION

Coming home. I find you still in bed,
but when I pull back the blanket,
I see your stomach is flat as an iron.
You've done it, as you warned me you would
and left the fetus wrapped in wax paper
for me to look at. My son.
Woman, loving you no matter what you do,

what can I say, except that I've heard
the poor have no children, just small people
and there is room only for one man in this house.

Lucille Clifton

THE LOST BABY POEM

the time i dropped your almost body down
down to meet the waters under the city
and run one with the sewage to the sea
what did i know about waters rushing back
what did i know about drowning
or being drowned

you would have been born into winter
in the year of the disconnected gas
and no car   we would have made the thin
walk over Genesee hill into the Canada wind
to watch you slip like ice into strangers' hands
you would have fallen naked as snow into winter
if you were here i could tell you these
and some other things

if i am ever less than a mountain
for your definite brothers and sisters
let the rivers pour over my head
let the sea take me for a spiller
of seas   let black men call me stranger
always   for your never named sake

Anne Sexton

THE ABORTION

Somebody who should have been born
is gone.

Just as the earth puckered its mouth,
each bud puffing out from its knot,
I changed my shoes, and then drove south.

Up past the Blue Mountains, where
Pennsylvania humps on endlessly,
wearing, like a crayoned cat, its green hair,

its roads sunken in like a gray washboard;
where, in truth, the ground cracks evilly,
a dark socket from which the coal has poured,

Somebody who should have been born
is gone.

the grass as bristly and stout as chives,
and me wondering when the ground would break,
and me wondering how anything fragile survives;

up in Pennsylvania, I met a little man,
not Rumpelstiltskin, at all, at all...
he took the fullness that love began.

Frank O'Hara

AN ABORTION

Do not bathe her in blood,
the little one whose sex is
undermined, she drops leafy
across the belly of black

sky and her abyss has not
that sweetness of the March
wind. Her conception ached
with the perversity of nursery
rhymes, she was a shad a
snake a sparrow and a girl's
closed eye. At the supper, weeping,
they said let's have her and
at breakfast: no.

Don't bathe
her in tears, guileless, beguiled
in her peripheral warmth, more
monster than murdered, safe
in all silences. From our tree
dropped, that she not wither,
autumn in our terrible breath.

Richard Jones

THE LULLABY

When she had the abortion
she didn't tell me.

She took a taxi to the clinic,
signed her name,

and waited with the other women
and one young girl who was sobbing.

That night she told me
she was tired.

She went to bed early
and turned on the fan —

its music helped her sleep –
and through its blades she heard me

singing
as I washed and put away the dishes.

Margo Bohanon

WOMAN

Strong Black women
are tin cans
in slimy gutters
children playing
kick around
on rainy afternoons.
their hands get rough
nostrils numb
scrubbing white linoleum floors
with milky ammonia water.
Loves grow stale
with bloody aborted children
and temporary promises
lost in wine bottle forgetfulness.
Strong women
sacrifice dreams
for thin veiled future hopes,
portraits of happiness
for beautiful strong faces,
that dissolve
in cloudy acid tears.

M. Z. Ribalow

ABORTION

Your tickertape chatter
offers candy compliments on
my wit, my great good humor.
Your frozen words crack and smoke,
dry ice bouncing off these white walls.
Your teeth grind out a seasick smile.

I know you mean well.
After all, you got the money.
You will leave these cool corridors
whispering to others how well I am taking it.
Someday you will marry a pleased virgin.
You will make the transition.

Inside I am scraped clean.
Oddly detached from your solicitous
grief, small waves of proud relief.
This jeering pain in my intestines
is far more real than your glazed
eyes, your reassuring TV voice.

I am pure as the sea, a wounded
mermaid you may no longer touch.
I have eaten my young. Devoured by
a scalpel proxy for three green bills.
I have bought my own barrenness.
Beware my flesh. Beware.

Someday I will bear children.
The doctors say I need have no doubts.
But I will never be eaten again.
I am not digestible.
I will stick in your throat,
choke you like a fish bone.

I conjured wet stains on those antiseptic
sheets. I will go home soon. Darling,
I will make you disintegrate.
My blood is dark red acid, and you,
my vampire who poured me this dead
life, you must drink it too.

Lucille Day

THE ABORTION

In my green gown I remembered
the moon as a skewed smile,
the precarious tilt of a sailboat
far from the pier.

It seemed I was always alone.
Now, strangely crowded –
twenty-four of us waiting
in a ten-bed ward –
I touched the shoulder
of the dark-haired girl
hunched next to me, crying.

I remembered the shrill
cry of a black-winged bird
I could not name
and the trail of a shooting star
burning to ash.

The seconal did not affect me.
They gave me more, intravenously,
until my knees began to shake.

I could not rest or sleep
that morning amid masked faces,
pain and the nightmarish whir

of a machine in the next room.

In the raw light I remembered
a house with no number,
paint peeling, windows boarded,
the last one on the street
in a dead-end dream.

Judith Minty

THE BABIES

Sometimes in the night I hear them, the unborn babies,
mewing like blind kittens: those boys
conceived behind steering wheels in dark, farmers' fields;
those girls pumped into life on borrowed beds.

Sometimes I see him, that doctor, scraping away
in the hotel room; the roasting pan carried as if it held
the Baptist's head; the toilet swallowing in anonymous gulps.

Oh Shirlie, Ann: Do you mourn them, as I do,
now when you cuddle your last aging baby to your breasts?

Acknowledgements

Every effort has been made to trace copyright holders in all copyright material in this book. The editor regrets if there has been any oversight and suggests the publisher be contacted in any such event. We gratefully acknowledge the following permissions:

Ai, 'Abortion', from *Cruelty*, Houghton Mifflin Co. Reprinted by permission of the publisher, copyright © Ai 1970, 1973. All rights reserved. 'The Expectant Father', from *Killing Floor*, Houghton Mifflin Co. Reprinted by permission of the publisher, copyright © Ai 1979. All rights reserved.

Mary Balazs, 'Pregnant Teenager on the Beach', reprinted from *Mississippi Valley Review*, copyright © Western Illinois University, 1979. Reprinted by permission of the Editor.

Lionel Basney, 'Awaiting the Birth', copyright © Lionel Basney 1993.

Beth Bentley, 'Birthing', from *Phone Calls from the Dead*, Ohio University Press. Reprinted by permission and copyright © Beth Bentley 1970.

Wendell Berry, 'A Child Unborn, the Coming Year', from *Sabbaths*, North Point Press, copyright © Wendell Berry 1987. Reprinted by permission of North Point Press, a division of Farrar, Straus & Giroux, Inc.

John Berryman, 'Hello', from *Collected Poems 1937–1971*, Faber and Faber Ltd. Reprinted by permission and copyright © the publisher 1989.

Suzette Bishop, 'Doctors Are Solving the Mystery of Miscarriage', reprinted from *The Little Magazine*. Reprinted by permission and copyright © Suzette Bishop 1991.

Chana Bloch, 'The Secret Life', reprinted from *Poetry*, copyright © Modern Poetry Association 1992. Reprinted by permission of the Editor of *Poetry*.

Margo Bohanon, 'Woman'. Reprinted by permission and copyright © Margo Bohanon 1977.

Catherine Brewton, 'Madonna', reprinted from *New York Quarterly*. Reprinted by permission of the Chairman of *New York Quarterly* Board, copyright © *New York Quarterly* 1988.

Gwendolyn Brooks, 'Jessie Mitchell's Mother' and 'The Mother', from *Blacks*, Third World Press, Chicago. Reprinted by permission and copyright © Gwendolyn Brooks 1991.

Michael Dennis Browne, 'Breech', from *You Won't Remember This*, Carnegie Mellon University Press. Reprinted by permission and copyright © the publisher 1992.

Kathryn Stripling Byer, 'Lullabye', reprinted from *Carolina Quarterly* and *Wildwood Flower*, Louisiana State University Press. Reprinted by permission of the publisher, copyright © Kathryn Stripling Byer 1992.

George Charlton, 'Morning Sickness', from *Nightshift Workers*, Bloodaxe Books. Reprinted by permission and copyright © the publisher 1989.

Helen Chasin, 'The Recovery Room: Lying in', from *Coming Close and Other Poems*, Yale University Press. Reprinted by permission and copyright © the publisher 1968.

Gillian Clarke, 'Scything' and 'Sheila Na Gig at Kilpeck', from *Letter from a Far Country*, Carcanet Press, Ltd. Reprinted by permission and copyright © the publisher 1982.

Lucille Clifton, 'the lost baby poem', from *good woman: poems and a memoir 1969–1980*, BOA Editions, Ltd. Reprinted by permission of BOA Editions, Ltd., 92 Park Avenue, Brockport, NY 14420 and Lucille Clifton, copyright © Lucille Clifton 1987.

Robert P. Cooke, 'When You Were Born' reprinted from the *Great Lakes Review* (now the *Michigan Historical Review*). Reprinted by permission and copyright © the *Michigan Historical Review* and Clarke Historical Library 1985.

J. William Corrington, 'For a Woodscolt Miscarried', reprinted from *Contemporary Poetry in America*, ed. Miller Williams 1973. Reprinted by permission of Joyce H. Corrington, Executor of the Estate of J. William Corrington, 1993.

Peter Dale, 'The Rite', from *Mortal Fire*, Agenda Editions. Reprinted by permission of the publisher, copyright © Peter Dale 1976.

Ann Darr, 'Oblique Birth Poem', Dryad Press. Reprinted by permission and copyright © Ann Darr 1978. 'Waiting', from *The Twelve Pound Cigarette*, SCOP Publishers. Reprinted by permission and copyright © Ann Darr 1990.

Lucille Day, 'The Abortion', from *Lookings and Listenings*, Alameda Poets' Fourth Anthology, Alameda Poets. Reprinted by permission and copyright © Lucille Day 1982. 'Labor', from *Poems*, Berkeley Poets Workshop and Press. Reprinted by permission and copyright © Lucille Day 1979.

Jill Dawson, 'The Crossing'. Reprinted by permission and copyright © Jill Dawson, 1992.

Barry Dempster, 'Mother', reprinted from *Sou'wester*, copyright © *Sou'wester* 1978. Reprinted by permission of the Editor.

Toi Derricotte, 'This Woman Will not Bear Children', from *New Poets: Women,* ed. Terry Wetherby, Les Femmes Publishing. Reprinted by permission and copyright © Toi Derricotte 1976.

Rosemary Dobson, 'The Birth', from *Collected Poems*, Angus & Robertson Bay Books. Reprinted by permission of the publisher, copyright © Rosemary Dobson 1992.

Gail Rudd Entrekin, 'This Time', copyright © Gail Rudd Entrekin 1993.

Mira Fish, 'Pregnancy', reprinted from *Flowering After Frost*, ed. Michael McMahon, Branden Publishing Boston. Reprinted by permission and copyright © the publisher 1975.

Linda Nemec Foster, 'Family Pose', reprinted from *Tendril*, 'The Man Dreams of His Pregnant Wife', and 'The Pregnant Woman Dreams of Herself', copyright © Linda Nemec Foster 1992.

Kathleen Fraser, 'Poems for the New', from *Change of Address and Other Poems*, Kayak Books 1966, and 'Poem Wondering If I'm Pregnant', from *In Defiance (of the Rains)*, Kayak Books 1969, copyright © Kathleen Fraser 1966, 1969. Reprinted by permission of Marian Reiner for the author.

David Galler, 'The Abortion', reprinted from *Prairie Schooner* by permission of the University of Nebraska Press, copyright © University of Nebraska Press 1991.

Sandra M. Gilbert, 'About the Beginning', reprinted from *Poetry*, copyright © The Modern Poetry Association 1991. Reprinted by permission of the Editor of *Poetry*.

Louise Glück, 'For My Mother', from *The House on Marshland*, The Ecco Press, 1975. Reprinted by permission of the publisher, copyright © Louise Glück 1971, 1972, 1973, 1974, 1975.

Lorna Goodison, 'Birth Stone', reprinted from *The Hudson Review*, Vol. XLIII, No. 4 (Winter 1991) by permission of *The Hudson Review*, copyright © Lorna Goodison 1991.

Mary Gordon, 'The Unwanted', reprinted from *The Little Magazine*. Reprinted by permission of Sterling Lord Literistic, copyright © Mary Gordon 1972.

Jorie Graham, 'Wanting a Child', from *Erosion*, Princeton University Press. Reprinted by permission and copyright © the publisher 1983.

Emily Grosholz, 'Fausse Couche', from *Shores and Headlands*, Princeton University Press. Reprinted by permission and copyright © the publisher 1988. 'Thirty-Six Weeks', reprinted from *Poetry*, copyright © The Modern Poetry Association 1991. Reprinted by permission of the Editor of *Poetry*.

Thom Gunn, 'Baby Song', from *Jack Straw's Castle and Other Poems*, Faber and Faber Ltd. Reprinted by permission and copyright © the publisher 1976.

Helena Hinn, '37 – 38 – 37', from *The Quickening*, copyright © Helen Hinn 1992.

Rachel Hadas, 'Amniocentesis', reprinted from *Prairie Schooner*, by permission of the University of Nebraska Press, copyright © University of Nebraska Press 1990.

Anne Halley, 'Against Dark's Harm' and 'O Doctor Dear My Love', from *Between Wars and*

Other Poems, Amherst: University of Massachusetts Press. Reprinted by permission and copyright © the publisher 1965.

Deborah Harding, 'Late', reprinted from *Michigan Quarterly Review*. Reprinted by permission and copyright © Deborah Harding 1991.

Michael S. Harper, 'The Borning Room', from *Song: I Want a Witness*, University of Pittsburgh Press. Reprinted by permission of the publisher, copyright © Michael S. Harper 1972.

Seamus Heaney, 'Mother', from *Poems 1965–1975*, Faber and Faber Ltd. Reprinted by permission of the publisher, copyright © Seamus Heaney 1980. 'A Pillowed Head', from *Seeing Things*, Faber and Faber Ltd. Reprinted by permission of the publisher, copyright © Seamus Heaney 1991. All rights reserved.

Anthony Hecht, 'The Vow', from *The Hard Hours*, Alfred A. Knopf, Inc. Reprinted by permission and copyright © the publisher 1967.

Judith Hemschemeyer, 'The Petals of the Tulips' and 'The Slaughter of the Innocents', from *The Ride Home*, Texas Tech University Press. Reprinted by permission and copyright © Judith Hemschemeyer 1987.

Geof Hewitt, 'Emergency at 8', from *Stone Soup*, Ithaca House. Reprinted by permission and copyright © Geof Hewitt 1974.

Helen Hoffman, 'Night Journey', reprinted from *The Ohio Review*. Reprinted by permission of the Editor of *The Ohio Review* and Helen Hoffman, copyright © Helen Hoffman 1984.

David Holbrook, 'Fingers in the Door' and 'Maternity Gown', from *Selected Poems*, Anvil Press. Reprinted by permission and copyright © David Holbrook 1980.

Jeremy Hooker, 'Birth', from *A View from the Source*, Carcanet Press, Ltd. Reprinted by permission and copyright © the publisher 1982.

Langston Hughes, translations of 'Image of the Earth' and 'Mother' by Gabriela Mistral. Reprinted by permission of Yale Collection of American Literature, Beinecke Rare Book and Manuscript Library, Yale University 1993.

Ted Hughes, 'Childbirth', from *The Hawk in the Rain*, Faber and Faber Ltd. Reprinted by permission of the publisher, copyright © Ted Hughes 1957.

Colette Inez, 'Waiting for the Doctor', from *The Woman Who Loved Worms*, Doubleday. Reprinted by permission and copyright © Colette Inez 1972.

David Jauss, 'For My Son, Born During an Ice Storm', reprinted from *Strings: A Gathering of Family Poems*, ed. Paul B. Janeczko, Bradbury Press. Reprinted by permission and copyright © David Jauss 1984.

Mike Jenkins, 'For Bethan', reprinted from *Anglo-Welsh Review*. Reprinted by permission and copyright © Mike Jenkins 1982, and 'The Mouth', copyright © Mike Jenkins 1993.

Elizabeth Jennings, 'The Unknown Child', from *Collected Poems 1953–1985*, Carcanet Press, Ltd. Reprinted by permission of David Higham Associates, copyright © Elizabeth Jennings 1986.

Bobi Jones, 'Portrait of a Pregnant Woman', from *Bobi Jones Selected Poems*, tr. Joseph P. Clancy, Christopher Davies Publishers Ltd. Reprinted by permission and copyright © the publisher 1987.

Richard Jones, 'The Lullaby' and 'White Towels', from *At Last We Enter Paradise*, Copper Canyon Press, copyright © Richard Jones 1991. Reprinted by permission of the author. 'The Miscarriage', from *Country of Air*, Copper Canyon Press, copyright © Richard Jones 1986. Reprinted by permission of the author.

Donald Justice, 'To a Ten Months' Child', from *The Summer Anniversaries*, Wesleyan University Press. Reprinted by permission and copyright © University Press of New England 1981.

Faye Kicknosway, 'In Mysterious Ways', from *All These Voices*, Coffee House Press. Reprinted by permission of the publisher, copyright © Faye Kicknosway 1986.

James Kirkup, 'To My Children Unknown Produced by Artificial Insemination', from *White Shadows, Black Shadows*, J. M. Dent. Reprinted by permission and copyright © James Kirkup 1992.

Steven Lautermilch, 'For My Wife', reprinted from *Centennial Review*. Reprinted by permission and copyright © Steven Lautermilch 1979.

Laurie Lee, 'Milkmaid', from *The Sun My Monument*, Chatto and Windus. Reprinted by permission and copyright © Peters Fraser & Dunlop Group Ltd. 1993.

Adelle Leiblein, 'Calling to the Soul of My Unborn Child', reprinted from *Nimrod*, Vol. 35.1, published by the Arts and Humanities Council of Tulsa. Reprinted by permission and copyright © Adelle Leiblein 1992.

Dorothy Livesay, 'Serenade for Strings', from *The Woman I Am*, Press Porcepic. Copyright © the publisher.

Audre Lorde, 'Father, the Year Is Fallen' and 'Now That I Am Forever with Child' from *Undersong*, Virago Press. Reprinted by permission and copyright © the publisher 1993. 'A Woman/Dirge for Wasted Children' from *Black Unicorn* 1978. Reprinted by permission of Abner Stein and W.W. Norton, copyright © Audre Lorde 1978.

Robert Lowell, 'Ninth Month', from *The Dolphin*, Faber and Faber Ltd. Reprinted by permission and copyright © the publisher 1973.

George Ella Lyon, 'Birth', reprinted from *Strings: A Gathering of Family Poems*, ed. Paul B. Janeczko, Bradbury Press. Reprinted by permission and copyright © George Ella Lyon 1984.

Mary McAnally, 'Our Mother's Body Is the Earth', reprinted from *Anima*, copyright © 1979. Reprinted by permission of the Editor.

Patricia McCarthy, 'Ante Natal Clinic', 'D and C', and 'Pregnancy After Forty'. Reprinted by permission and copyright © Patricia McCarthy 1993. 'Love-Child', reprinted from *A Second Skin*, Peterloo Poets. Reprinted by permission and copyright © the publisher 1985.

Hugh MacDiarmid, 'Lo a Child Is Born', from *Collected Poems*, Macmillan. Copyright © the publisher 1962.

Mark S. McLeod, 'Mother and Son', reprinted from *Rolling Coulter* Spring 1991. Reprinted by permission and copyright © Mark S. McLeod 1991.

Louis MacNeice, 'Prayer Before Birth', from *Collected Poems*, ed. E. R. Dodds. Reprinted by permission and copyright © David Higham Associates 1993.

Sandra McPherson, 'Pregnancy', from *Elegies for the Hot Season*, The Ecco Press. Reprinted by permission and copyright © the publisher 1982.

Andrew L. March, 'The Reversal of the Arrow of Time', reprinted from *Kansas Quarterly*. Reprinted by permission of the Editor of *Kansas Quarterly* and Andrew L. March, copyright © Andrew L. March 1990.

James Merrill, 'A Timepiece', from *Selected Poems 1946–1985*, Alfred A. Knopf, Inc. Reprinted with permission of the publisher, copyright © James Merrill 1992.

Vassar Miller, 'On Approaching My Birthday' from *Onions and Roses*, 1968, and 'Spinster's Lullaby', from *My Bones Being Wiser*, 1963, Wesleyan University Press. Reprinted by permission and copyright © University Press of New England 1963, 1968.

Helena Minton, 'God, Woman, Egg' and 'The Womb Is Ruins', from *Flowering After Frost*, ed. Michael McMahon, Branden Publishing Boston. Reprinted by permission and copyright © the publisher 1975.

Judith Minty, 'The Babies', from *Lake Songs and Other Fears*, University of Pittsburgh Press. Reprinted by permission and copyright © Judith Minty 1974. 'Letters to My Daughters #15', from *Dancing the Fault*, University of Central Florida Press. Reprinted by permission and copyright © the publisher 1991. 'Wounds', from *In the Presence of Mothers*, University of Pittsburgh Press. Reprinted by permission and copyright © Judith Minty 1981.

Stephen Mitchell, translation of 'Birth' by Amir Gilboa, reprinted from *Voices Within the Ark*,

Linda Pastan, 'Mother Eve', from *The Imperfect Paradise*, W. W. Norton. Reprinted by permission of the publisher and author, copyright © Linda Pastan 1988; 'Notes from the Delivery Room', from *PM/AM, New and Selected Poems*, W. W. Norton. Reprinted by permission of the publisher and author, copyright © Linda Pastan 1982.

Miriam Pederson, 'Acclimation', copyright © Miriam Pederson 1992. 'Erosion', from *Woman Poet: The Midwest*, Women in Literature, Inc. Reprinted by permission and copyright © the publisher 1985.

Paul Petrie, 'The Lost Child', reprinted from *Commonweal*. Reprinted by permission of the Editor of *Commonweal*, copyright © Commonweal Foundation 1984.

Sylvia Plath, 'Morning Song', from *Collected Poems*, ed. Ted Hughes, Faber and Faber Ltd. Reprinted by permission of the publisher, copyright © the Estate of Sylvia Plath 1960, 1965, 1971, 1981.

Barbara Ras, 'Pregnant Poets Swim Lake Tarleton, New Hampshire', reprinted from *The Massachusetts Review*. Reprinted by permission and copyright © *The Massachusetts Review* 1988.

Peter Redgrove, 'The Eggs', from *The Apple Broadcast*, Routledge and Kegan Paul, copyright © Peter Redgrove. Reprinted by permission of David Higham Associates.

M. Z. Ribalow, 'Abortion', reprinted from *New York Quarterly*. Reprinted by permission of the Chairman of *New York Quarterly* Board, copyright © *New York Quarterly* 1988.

Adrienne Rich, 'The Mirror in Which Two Are Seen as One', from *The Fact of a Doorframe, Poems Selected and New, 1950–1984*, W. W. Norton. Reprinted by permission of the publisher, copyright © 1975, 1978; copyright © Adrienne Rich 1981, 1984.

Anne Ridler, 'Christmas and Common Birth', from *The Nine Bright Shiners*, Faber and Faber Ltd. Reprinted by permission and copyright © the publisher 1943.

Kirk Robertson, 'Postcard to a Foetus', from *Under the Weight of the Sky*, Cherry Valley Editions, copyright © Kirk Robertson 1977.

Dafydd Rowlands, 'I Will Show You Beauty', from *Poetry of Wales 1930–1970*, ed. R. Gerallt Jones, Gomer Press. Reprinted by permission and copyright © the publisher 1974.

Muriel Rukeyser, 'Night Feeding', from *The Complete Poems of Muriel Rukeyser*, McGraw-Hill, copyright © Muriel Rukeyser 1978. Reprinted by permission of William L. Rukeyser.

Mary Jo Salter, 'Expectancy', from *Henry Purcell in Japan*, Alfred A. Knopf, Inc. Reprinted by permission of the publisher, copyright © Mary Jo Salter 1984.

Sally Harris Sange, 'Epithalamium' reprinted from *Kenyon Review*, – New Series, Fall 1992, Vol. XIV, No. 4, copyright © Kenyon College 1992. Reprinted by permission and copyright © Sally Harris Sange 1984.

Biographical Notes

Ai American

Describing herself as $\frac{1}{2}$ Japanese, $\frac{1}{8}$ Choctaw, $\frac{1}{4}$ Black, $\frac{1}{16}$ Irish, she is the author of several books of poetry including *Cruelty* and *Killing Floor* (which won the Lamont Poetry Award); her most recent book is *Fate: New Poems*. She is the recipient of a number of awards including a Guggenheim fellowship.

Mary Balazs American
Author of three volumes of poetry, *Out of Darkness, The Voice of Thy Brother's Blood* and *The Stones Refuse Their Peace*, her poems appear frequently in journals.

Lionel Basney American
Professor of English at Calvin College, his poems have appeared in *Shenandoah, Nimrod, Cumberland Poetry Review*, and in many other journals.

Beth Bentley American
She has recently edited *Hazel Hall: Selected Poems*.

Wendell Berry American
Professor of English at the University of Kentucky, he is essaysit, novelist, and poet; among his books of poetry are *Sabbaths, The Wheel*, and *The Unforeseen Wilderness*. He is the recipient of many awards including a Guggenheim fellowship, a Rockefeller grant, and a National Institute of Arts and Letters award.

John Berryman American
Essayist and poet, he is best known for *The Dream Songs*, a sequence of 385 poems which caused critics to compare him with Homer, Dante, and Whitman. He was the recipient of many awards including the Pulitzer Prize, the Bollingen Award, a Guggenheim fellowship, and the Harriet Monroe Poetry Award.

Suzette Bishop American
Teacher in Tulsa, Oklahoma, her poems have appeared in a number of journals.

Chana Bloch American
Professor of English at Mills College, she is author of two books of poetry, *The Secrets of the Tribe* and *The Past Keeps Changing*, and of a critical study on George Herbert, *Spelling the Word: George Herbert and the Bible*. Forthcoming is her translation (with Ariel Bloch) of *Song of Songs*.

Margo Bohanon American
Teacher at Cuyahoga Community College, her poems have appeared in a number of journals.

Gwendolyn Brooks American
Recipient of two Guggenheim fellowships, a grant from the National Institute of Arts and Letters, and the Pulitzer Prize for her second book of poems, she was named 'Poet Laureate of the State of Illinois' in 1969. Author of a number of volumes of poetry including *A Street in Bronzeville, The Bean Eaters,* and *To Disembark,* she has also written novels and an autobiography, *Report from Part One.*

Michael Dennis Browne American
Director of the Program in Creative and Professional Writing at the University of Minnesota, he is the author of several books of poetry including *The Wife of Winter, Smoke from the Fires,* and *You Won't Remember This.*

Kathryn Stripling Byer American
A poet-in-resident at Western Carolina University, her second book, *Wildwood Flower,* was named the 1992 Lamont Poetry Selection of the Academy of American Poets.

George Charlton British
He is the author of a book of poems, *Nightshift Workers.*

Helen Chasin American
She has recently edited Qui Baishi, *Likeness and Unlikeness: Selected Paintings.*

Gillian Clarke Welsh
Free-lance lecturer, writier, BBC news researcher and broadcaster, she has been the recipient of travel grants to Ireland, the Soviet Union, Yugoslavia, and the United States. Her books of poems include *The Sundial* (winner of the Welsh Arts Council poetry prize) and *Letter from a Far Country.*

Lucille Clifton American
The recipient of the University of Massachusetts Press's Juniper Prize for Poetry, an Emmy Award from the American Academy of Television Arts and Sciences, and creative writing fellowships from NEA, her works include *An Ordinary Woman, Two-Headed Woman,* and *Sonora Beautiful.* She has also written a number of books for children.

Robert P. Cooke American
Holder of an MFA from the University of Oregon, he has been a pipefitter and welder at the Amoco, Whiting, Refinery.

J. William Corrington American
Lawyer, Professor of English, television and film writer (frequently collaborating with his wife, Joyce, on scripts), novelist, and poet, he won the Charioteer Poetry Prize for *Where We Are,* and an NEA award for a short story. His novels include *The Upper Hand* and *The Man Who Slept with Women.*

Peter Dale British
Editor of *Agenda*, he is author of several books of poetry including a sonnet sequence, *One Another*.

Ann Darr American
A pilot in the American Airforce in WWII, her books of poetry include *Cleared for Landing*, *Do You Take This Woman?*, and *Riding with the Fireworks*.

Jill Dawson British
Has contributed to various books and anthologies, editor of the *Virago Book of Wicked Verse*. Was awarded an Eric Gregory Award for her poetry in 1992.

Lucille Day American
Director of the Hall of Health, a hands-on health museum in Berkeley, California, her poems have appeared in *The Hudson Review*, *The Threepenny Review*, and other journals. Her first poetry collection, *Self-Portrait with Hand Microscope* received the Henry Jackson Award from the San Francisco Foundation.

Barry Dempster Canadian
Poet and novelist, he is a frequent contributor of poetry to journals; his volumes of poetry include *Fables for Isolated Men*, *Positions to Pray In*, and *The Unavoidable Man*.

Toi Derricotte American
Guest poet and lecturer at colleges and universities, she is frequently featured as a poet in readings at theatres, museums, and libraries. She has received many awards including grants from the Academy of American Poets, the MacDowell Colony, NEA, and the Lucille Medmick Memorial Award from the Poetry Society of America. Her books of poetry include *Captivity* and *The Empress of the Death House*.

Rosemary Dobson Australian
The recipient of awards from the Sydney *Morning Herald*, grants from the Australia Council Literary Board, and the Myer Award, she is the author of several volumes of poetry including *The Ship of Ice and Other Poems* and *Selected Poems*.

Gail Rudd Entrekin American
Editor and production manager for the Berkeley Poets Workshop & Press, she teaches English at Diablo Valley College. Her poems won Honorable Mention in the 1992 Wildwood Poetry Prize Competition and were finalists for the 1991 New Letters Literary Awards. *You Notice the Body* was a finalist in both the Rainmaker Awards and Bluestem Awards competitions.

Linda Nemec Foster American
Her poems have appeared in many journals including *The Georgia Review*, *Negative Capability*, and *Nimrod*; she is author of a chapbook, *A History of the Body*.

Kathleen Fraser American
Professor of English at San Francisco State University who divides her time between

San Francisco and Rome, she is the author of several books of poetry. Her *Collected Poems, 1966-1992* is due out in Spring 1994 from the National Poetry Foundation.

David Galler American
His poems appear frequently in journals including *TriQuarterly Magazine* and *Southwest Review*; he is currently working on a fourth poetry collection.

Sandra Gilbert American
Professor of English at the University of California, Davis, she is co-winner of the 1990 Charity Randall Prize from the International Poetry Forum; her books of poetry include *Blood Pressure* and *Emily's Bread*. She is co-author with Susan Gubar of *No Man's Land* and *The Madwoman in the Attic*.

Amir Gilboa Russian
Poet and Editor, he immigrated illegally to Israel in 1937 where he took up poetry as a vocation. The recipient of many awards including the Bialik Award and the Bertha and Irving Neuman Hebrew Literary Award (posthumously in 1984), he is the author of *Light of the Last Suns*, a volume of poetry translated into English.

Louise Glück American
Author of several books of poetry including *Firstborn, The House on Marshland, The Garden* and *Descending Figure*, she won the Pulitzer Prize for her most recent book, *The Wild Iris*.

Lorna Goodison Jamaican
Her new anthology, *Selected Poems*, evokes a lineage of strong female figures and of family and motherhood; earlier volumes of poetry include *I Am Becoming My Mother* and *Heartease*.

Mary Gordon American
Essayist and poet, she is best known for her fiction; her novels include *The Company of Women, Final Payments*, and *The Other Side*.

Jorie Graham American
Professor of English at the University of Iowa, she has been a Guggenheim fellow and the recipient of a John D. and Catherine T. MacArthur Foundation fellowship. Her books of poetry include *Erosion* and *Region of Unlikeness*. She is editor of *The Best American Poetry 1990*.

Emily Grosholz American
Professor of Philosophy at Penn State University, she has received an Ingram Merrill Award and a Guggenheim Fellowship for poetry. Her most recent book of poetry is *Eden*.

Thom Gunn British
The recipient of many awards including a Guggenheim fellowship, the Levinson Prize, and a Rockefeller Award, he is the author of a number of books of poetry

including *Jack Straw's Castle, The Man with Night Sweats* and *The Passages of Joy*.

Rachel Hadas American
Professor of English at Rutgers Univeristy, she has been awarded the Ann Stanford Poetry Prize; she is the author of *Pass It On* and *Slow Transparency*. Her most recent project is *Unending Dialogue: Voices from AIDS Poetry Workshop*.

Anne Halley American
Poet and novelist, she is co-editor of *The Massachusetts Review*. The recipient of several awards including a Longview Award and the Massachusetts Artists Foundation Award, her volumes of poetry include *Betweeen Wars and Other Poems, Rumors of the Turning Wheel*, and her most recent book, *The Bearded Mother*.

Deborah Harding American
A teacher in San Diego, her poems appear frequently in journals including *The Antioch Review* and *Kansas Quarterly*.

Michael Harper American
Professor of English and Director of the Writing Program at Brown University, he is the author of several books of poetry including *Dear John, Dear Coltrane, Healing Song for the Inner Bar*, and *Nightmare Begins Responsibility*.

Seamus Heaney Irish
Professor of Poetry at the University of Oxford and Boylston Professor of Rhetoric and Oratory at Harvard University, he is author of a number of books of poetry including *Station Island, The Haw Lantern* and *Seeing Things*. He is the recipient of many awards including the Lannan Literary Award, the W.H. Smith Award, the Duff Cooper Memorial Prize, and grants from Fordham University and Queen's University of Belfast.

Helena Hinn British
A trained librarian, her poems have been widely anthologised. Her volume of poetry, *The Quickening* has yet to be published.

Anthony Hecht American
Professor in the Graduate School of Georgetown University, he is author of a number of books of poetry including *The Venetian Vespers, Millions of Strange Shadows*, and *The Transparent Man*. He is the recipient of many awards including the Ruth Lilly Poetry Prize, a Prix de Rome fellowship, a Guggenheim fellowship, and the Pulitzer Prize for *The Hard Hours*.

Judith Hemschemeyer American
Professor of English at the University of Central Florida, she is the author of *The Ride Home* and *Very Close and Very Slow*, and the translator of the poetry of Anna Akhmatova.

Geof Hewitt American
He is the author of *Just Worlds* and *Stone Soup*.

Helen Hoffman American
Former Coordinator of the Writers' Center at the Race Street Gallery, Grand
Rapids, Michigan, her poems appear frequently in journals.

David Holbrook British
An Emeritus Fellow of Downing College, Cambridge, he is the author of novels,
books on education, criticism, and a number of books of poetry including *Moments
in Italy* and *Old World New World*.

Jeremy Hooker British
Author of *Poetry of Place*, a collection of essays on poetry and fiction, his books of
poetry include *Solent Short* and *Landscape of the Daylight Moon*.

Langston Hughes American
Translator of the poems of Gabriela Mistral, he is the author of a number of
volumes of poetry, fiction, and essays, and editor of *Best Short Stories of Negro Writers*
and *Pictorial History of Black Americans*. His papers are in the Beinecke Rare Book
and Manuscript Library, Yale University.

Ted Hughes British
The recipient of many prizes and awards, he was appointed England's Poet Laureate
in 1984. He is the author of a number of volumes of poetry including *Hawk in the
Rain*, *River*, and *Wolfwatching*. Several of his books of poems have been illustrated
by Leonard Baskin.

Colette Inez American
Poet-in-the-Schools and Lecturer-in-Poetry at colleges, universities, and libraries, she
is the author of a number of books of poetry including *Eight Minutes from the Sun* and
Family Life. Her awards include a grant from NEA, a National League of American
Pen Women Poetry Award, and awards from the Poetry Society of America.

David Jauss American
Professor of English and Director of the Creative Writing Program at the
University of Arkansas, he has received the O. Henry Award and Pushcart Prize.
He is the Editor of *The Best of Crazyhorse: Thirty Years of Poetry and Fiction* and Co-
Editor of *Strong Measures: Contemporary American Poetry in Traditional Forms*.

Mike Jenkins Welsh
The author of several books of poetry, his second book, *Empire of Smoke*, won the
Welsh Arts Council Young Writers Prize.

Elizabeth Jennings British
She is the author of more than a dozen books of poetry including *Moments of Grace*,
Celebrations and Elegies, and *Extending the Territory*.

Bobi Jones Welsh
A member of the Welsh Department at the University College of Wales, Aberystwyth, he has written novels, short stories, and criticism. His volumes of poetry include *Bwyta'n Te, Rhwng Taf a Thaf, Allor Wydn*, and *Selected Poems*.

Richard Jones American
The Editor of *Poetry East*, he teaches at DePaul University. He is the author of *Country of Air* and, most recently, *At Last We Enter Paradise*.

Donald Justice American
The author of a number of volumes of poetry including *Night Light* and *The Summer Anniversaries* (which won the Lamont Award of the Academy of American Poets), he won the Pulitzer Prize for poetry in 1980; he is also the author of a book of criticism, *Platonic Scripts*, in the Poets on Poetry series.

Faye Kicknosway American
She is the author of several volumes of poetry including *She Wears Him Fancy in Her Night Braid* and *All These Voices: New and Selected Poems*.

James Kirkup British
The recipient of many awards including the Atlantic Award in Literature from the Rockefeller Foundation, the International Literary Prize, Japan P.E.N., and the Keats Prize of Poetry, his volumes of poetry include *The Submerged Village and Other Poems* and *Paper Window: Poems from Japan*.

Steven Lautermilch American
He teaches at the University of North Carolina, Greensboro, and publishes poetry and photographs.

Laurie Lee British
The author of an autobiography, *Cider with Rosie*, his volumes of poetry include *the Bloom of Candles* and *The Voyage of Magellan*.

Adelle Leiblein American
A holder of a residency/fellowship at the Wurlitzer Foundation in Taos, New Mexico, in the 1980s, she has taught writing at the Worcester Art Museum and elsewhere. Her poem 'Calling to the Soul of My Unborn Child' was a Pushcart Prize nominee in 1992 and received first honourable mention in the Neruda Prize Competition; her poems have appeared in a number of journals including *Nimrod, Red Brick Review*, and *The Denver Quarterly*.

Dorothy Livesay Canadian
The recipient of numerous awards including two Governor-General's Awards for Poetry and the Governor-General's Persons Award (given to outstanding Canadian women), the Queen's Canada Medal, a Canada Council fellowship and Senior Arts grant, and the subject of a documentary film (*The Woman I Am*), her volumes of poetry include *Nine Poems of Farewell 1972-1973, Ice Age*, and *The Woman I am*. She

is the author of a volume of short stories, *A Winnipeg Childhood*, and of an autobiography, *Right Hand Left Hand*.

Audre Lorde American
She is the author of many volumes of poetry including *Chosen Poems Old and New*, *Cables to Rage*, and *Zami: A New Spelling of My Name*. The recipient of many awards including NEA grants and Creative Artists Public Service grants, her last work was *Cancer Journals*.

Robert Lowell American
The recipient of the Pulitzer Prize, the National Book Award, the Bollingen Poetry Translation Award, the Copernicus Award, and the National Book Critics Circle Award, his volumes of poetry - which he described as 'my autobiography in verse' - include *Life Studies*, *For the Union Dead*, *The Dolphin*, and *Day by Day*.

George Ella Lyon American
The author of a book of poetry, *Moving Out*, she is also the author of a number of children's books including *Cecil's Story*, *Basket*, and *Dreamplace*.

Mary McAnally American
Author of *The Absence of the Father and the Dance of Zygotes*, she is also Editor of *Warning: Anthology of Poetry from Prisoners of Oklahoma*.

Patricia McCarthy British
A frequent contributor to journals and the author of *A Second Skin*, her poem 'Pregnancy after Forty' won the Kent and Sussex Poetry competition; she is preparing another volume of poetry for publication.

Mark S. McLeod American
Professor of Philosophy at the University of Texas at San Antonio, his poetry appears in a number of journals.

Sandra McPherson American
Director of the Creative Writing Program at the University of California, Davis, she is the recipient of a Guggenheim fellowship and an NEA grant; her volumes of poetry include *Floralia*, *The Year of Our Birth* and *Streamers*.

Hugh MacDiarmid Scottish
Writing under the pseudonym Christopher Murray Grieve, he was both poet and critic; his *Complete Poems 1920-1976* appeared posthumously in 1978.

Louis MacNeice British
Dramatist, novelist, and poet, his books of poetry include *The Earth Compels*, *Holes in the Sky*, and *The Burning Perch*; his autobiography, *The Strings Are False*, appeared posthumously in 1965.

Andrew L. March American
He is co-author of a number of books including *Gourmet Introduction to the Best*

Common Mushrooms of the Southern Rocky Mountains. . . . and *The Quest for Wild Jelly.*

James Merrill American
He is the author of a number of volumes of poetry including *The Changing Light at Sandover* and *From the First Nine.* He was awarded the Rebekah Johnson Bobbitt National Prize for Poetry given by the Library of Congress for *The Inner Room,* the National Book Award for *Nights and Days* and *Mirabell,* the Bollingen Prize for *Braving the Elements,* and the Pulitzer Prize for *Divine Comedies.*

Vassar Miller American
She is the author of a number of volumes of poetry including *If I Could Sleep Deeply Enough* and *If I Had Wheels or Love: Collected Poems of Vassar Miller;* she is also the Editor of *Despite This Flesh: The Disabled in Stories and Poems.*

Helena Minton American
She is the author of a book of poems, *The Canal Bed.*

Judith Minty American
Professor of English and Director of the Creative Writing Program at Humboldt State University of California, she is the author of a number of volumes of poetry including *In the Presence of Mothers, Lake Songs and Other Fears,* and the most recently published, *Dancing the Fault.*

Gabriela Mistral Chilean
The recipient of many awards, including the Juegos Florales laurel crown and gold medal from the city of Santiago, Chile, in 1914, she received the Nobel Prize for Literature in 1945. She served in the consuls in Italy, Spain, Portugal, Brazil, and the United States.

Stephen Mitchell American
He is the translator of many books including *The Book of Job, The Gospel According to Jesus: A New Translation and Guide to His Essential Teachings for Believers and Unbelievers,* and *Tao Te Ching: A New English Version.*

Lisel Mueller American
She is the author of two chapbooks and five collections of poetry, the most recent of which is *Waving from Shore;* in 1981 she won the National Book Award for *The Need to Hold Still.*

Joan Rohr Myers American
Her poems appear frequently in journals including *Christian Century* and *Commonweal.*

Kim Nam-Jo Korean
A teacher at Sukmyong Women's University, Korea, she won the Korea Free Literature Association Prize in 1958. Included in the number of volumes of poetry she has written is *The Flag of Mind.*

John Frederick Nims American
He is the author of a number of volumes of poetry including *The Six-Cornered Snowflake and Other Poems* and *Zany in Denim,* of a book of essays, *A Local Habitation: Essays on Poetry,* and the translator of *Sappho to Valery.*

Christopher Nye American
He is the Chair of the Sciences and Engineering Department of Berkshire Community College and a frequent contributor of poetry to journals.

Joyce Carol Oates American
Poet, novelist, short story writer, dramatist, and essayist, her most recent fiction is *Black Water* (novel) and *Where Is Here?* (short stories); her volumes of poetry include *Women in Love and Other Poems* and *Women Whose Lives Are Food, Men Whose Lives Are Money.*

Frank O'Hara American
A Curator for the Museum of Modern Art, he also worked for two years at *Art News;* he was at the centre of the Abstract Expressionist movement. His *Collected Poems* appeared posthumously in 1980.

Sharon Olds American
The author of several volumes of poetry including The Dead and the Living, The Gold Cell, and *The Father,* she is the recipient of a Lila Acheson Wallace-Readers Digest Fund Fellowship for 1993-96.

Amy Olson-Binder American
She is a free-lance writer who is currently working on the development of electronic kits for schools in California.

Alicia Suskin Ostriker American
Professor of English at Rutgers University, she is the author of a number of books of poetry including *The Imaginary Lover* (which won the William Carlos Williams prize in 1986) and *Green Age;* her new critical book is *Feminist Revision and the Bible.* She is currently working on a poetry sequence, *The Mastectomy Poems.*

Charlotte Otten American
A frequent contributor to journals, her poems have appeared in *The South Florida Poetry Review, The Southern Humanities Review, Interim,* and many others; her book of poems for children, *Months,* is forthcoming. Editor of *A Lycanthropy Reader: Werewolves in Western Culture,* her most recent book is *English Women's Voices, 1540-1700.*

Robert Pack American
Professor of English at Middlebury College and Director of the Breadloaf Writers Conference, he is the author of a number of volumes of poetry including his most recent *Before It Vanishes: A Packet for Professor Pagels.* His *The Long View* is a collection of essays as well as an autobiography.

Greg Pape American
He is the author of several volumes of poetry including *The Morning Horse, Border Crossings,* and *Black Branches.*

Linda Pastan American
The poet laureate of Maryland, she is the author of eight volumes of poetry, the most recent of which is *Heroes in Disguise.*

Miriam Pederson American
A teacher of creative writing at Aquinas College, she is a frequent contributor to journals; her poems recently won an award by *The MacGuffin.* She has co-authored with Ron Pederson a chapbook of poetry and sculpture, *The Adding We Do in Our Sleep.*

Paul Petrie American
He is the author of several volumes of poetry including *Light from the Furnace Rising, Not Seeing Is Believing,* and *Strange Gravity: Songs Physical and Metaphysical.*

Sylvia Plath American
The author of the autobiographical novel, *The Bell Jar,* her first poem appeared when she was eight years old. Author of *The Colossus, Ariel, Crossing the Water: Transitional Poems,* and other volumes of poetry, the *Collected Poems: Sylvia Plath,* edited by Ted Hughes, appeared posthumously in 1981. Her papers are in the Lilly Library, Indiana University, and the Neilson Library, Smith College.

Barbara Ras American
An editor at the University of California Press, her poems appear frequently in journals.

Peter Redgrove British
Poet, novelist, and scientific journalist, he is the author of many volumes of poetry including *The Force and Other Poems, Sons of My Skin: Selected Poems 1954-74,* and *The Weddings at Nether Powers.* His novels include *In the Country of the Skin* and *The Beekeepers.*

M. Z. Ribalow American
Professor of Communications at Fordham University, her poems have appeared in a number of journals.

Adrienne Rich American
Recipient of many honours including awards from the Guggenheim and Ingram Merrill Foundations, a commission from the Bollingen Foundation, and the 1991 Common Wealth Award in Literature, her most recent book (her thirteenth book of poetry), *An Atlas of the Difficult World,* received the Lenore Marshall-National award and the Los Angeles Times Book Award for poetry. Her prose writings include *Of Woman Born: Motherhood as Experience and Institution* and *Women and Honor: Some Notes on Lying.*

Anne Ridler British
The recipient of a number of awards including the Oscar Blumenthal Prize and the Union League Civic and Arts Foundation Prize, her books of poetry include *The Golden Bird and Other Poems* and *A Matter of Life and Death.* She is the translator of operatic libretti and the Editor of *Best Ghost Stories* and *Best Stories of Church and Clergy.*

Kirk Robertson American
He is the author of several volumes of poetry including *Driving to Vegas: New and Selected Poems 1969-1987, Two Weeks Off,* and *Matters of Equal Height.*

Dafydd Rowlands Welsh
Lecturer in Welsh at Trinity College, Carmarthen, he has twice won the crown at the National Eisteddford, in 1969, and 1972. Written in Welsh, his volumes of poetry include *Meini.*

Muriel Rukeyser American
Poet and biographer, her complete poetry, *The Collected Poems of Muriel Rukeyser,* appeared in 1978; her biographies include *Willard Gibbs, One Life* and *The Traces of Thomas Hariot.*

Mary Jo Salter American
Poet-in-Residence at Robert Frost Place and Instructor in English Conversation in Japanese institutions 1980-83, she is the recipient of the Discovery Prize from *Nation* and of an NAE fellowship. Her poems appear in a number of journals including *The New Yorker, Poetry,* and *The Kenyon Review.*

Sally Harris Sange American
A physician in Merritt Island, Florida, her poems appear frequently in journals.

Armand Schwerner American
Adapter and translator of poems from Native American, Yiddish, and French, he is Professor of English at the College of Staten Island, CUNY. His books of poetry include *The Lightfall, The Tablets I-XXVI,* and *Seaweed.*

Anne Sexton American
The author of eight volumes of poetry including *To Bedlam and Part Way Back, All My Pretty Ones,* and *The Awful Rowing Toward God (The Complete Poems* includes posthumously published work), she was the recipient of many awards including the Pulitzer Prize and the Shelley Memorial Prize from the Poetry Society of America. She was elected a fellow of the Royal Society of Literature in London.

Carol Shields Canadian
Poet and novelist, she is the recipient of several awards including the Young Writers' Contest of the Canadian Broadcasting Company, Canada Council grants, and a fiction prize from the Canadian Authors Association. She is the author of a book of poetry, *Intersect,* and of novels *Mary Swann, Happenstance* and *The Republic of Love.*

Matt Simpson British
Senior Lecturer in English and Director of writing workshops, he frequently appears as a featured poet at poetry readings. His books of poetry include *Letters to Berlin, Uneasy Vespers,* and his latest, *An Elegy for the Galosherman - New and Selected Poems.*

Myra Sklarew American
Trained as a biologist, she was a research assistant at Yale University School of Medicine, Department of Neurophysiology; she also participated in seminars in the Cell Biology of Immunity at the National Institutes of Health. Professor and Co-Director of the MFA Program in Creative Writing in the Department of Literature at The American University, her publications (in a wide variety of fields) number in the hundreds and include volumes of poetry; *From the Backyard of the Diaspora* (which won the Jewish Book Council Award in Poetry), *The Science of Goodbyes,* and *Altamira.*

Ken Smith British
Poet and critic, his poems have appeared in a number of journals; his critical writing includes *The Changing Past: Trends in South African Historical Writing.*

W. D. Snodgrass American
The recipient of a number of awards including fellowships from the Guggenheim and Ingram Merrill foundations, the Academy of American Poets, and the National Institute of Arts and Letters, his first book of poems won the Pulitzer Prize in 1960. His books of poetry include *After Experience, If Birds Build with Your Hair, and Remains.*

Gary Snyder American
The recipient of a number of awards including a Bollingen grant for Buddhist Studies, a grant from the National Institute of Arts and Letters, and a Guggenheim fellowship, he was awarded the Pulitzer Prize in 1975. His books of poetry include *Myths and Texts, The Back Country, Turtle Island* (winner of the National Book Award), and *Axe Handles.*

Judith Sornberger American
Visiting Professor in Women's Studies at the University of Colorado, her poems have appeared in a number of journals including *Bloomsbury Review, Laurel Review,* and *Calyx;* she is Editor of *All My Grandmothers Could Sing, Poems by Nebraska Women.*

Helen Sorrells American
The recipient of many awards including grants from NEA, the Poetry Society of American Authors, and the Borestone Award, she is the author of several books of poetry including *Seeds As They Fall.*

Gary Soto American
Professor of English and Chicano Studies at the University of California, Berkeley, he is the recipient of an NEA Creative Writing Fellowship. His latest book of poems is *Home Course in Religion;* he is author of a book of essays, *A Summer Life.*

Jon Stallworthy British
Poet, editor, and translator, he is the recipient of many awards including the Newdigate Prize for English Verse, the Duff Cooper Memorial Prize, and the W. H. Smith and Son Literary Award. His volumes of poetry include *The Astronomy of Love, Out of Bounds,* and *Root and Branch;* he is the editor of the *Penguin Book of Love Poetry.*

C. K. Stead New Zealander
Poet, critic, and novelist, he is Professor of English at the University of Auckland. His critical writings include *The New Poetic: Yeats to Eliot* and *Pound, Yeats, Eliot and the Modernist Movement.* His most recent novel is *The End of the Century at the End of the World.*

Anne Stevenson British
The recipient of a number of fellowships including those from Dundee, Oxford, Reading, Newcastle, and Radcliffe, she is Writer-in-Residence at the University of Edinburgh. Her books of poetry include *Minute by Glass Minute, The Fiction-Makers,* and *Selected Poems.* She has written critical works on Elizabeth Bishop and Sylvia Plath.

John Stone American
Professor at the Emory University School of Medicine, he is the author of several books of poetry including *In All This Rain* and *Renaming the Streets,* and of essays on medicine, *In the Country of Hearts: Journeys in the Art of Medicine.*

Ruth Stone American
Professor of English at the State Univeristy of New York, Binghamton, she is the author of several books of poetry including *Second Hand Coat, The Solution,* and *Who Is the Widow's Muse?*

Alfonsina Storni Argentinian
An educator who worked for children's theatre, she was a foremost twentieth-century South American poet whose poems reveal her desire for equality of the sexes and the rights of women.

Linda Taylor American
Teacher of Literature and Writing at Oglethorpe University, her poems have appeared in a number of journals including *Poetry Northwest, The Kenyon Review,* and *Tar River Review;* she is author of a book on Henry James.

R. S. Thomas Welsh
Poet and clergyman, he is author of a number of volumes of poetry including *Song*

at the Year's Turning, Tares, and *The Echoes Return Slow;* he has edited *The Penguin Book of Religious Verse* and selections from Edward Thomas, George Herbert, and William Wordsworth.

Anthony Thwaite British
Poet and critic, he has been a producer for the BBC, literary editor of *The Listener,* and Co-editor of *Encounter.* His volumes of poetry include *Home Truths, The Stones of Emptiness,* and *A Portion for Foxes.* He is Editor of a collection of dramatic monologues, *Victorian Voices.*

Constance Urdang American
Poet and novelist, she is author of a book of poems, *Alternative Lives,* and of two novellas, *The Woman Who Read Novels* and *Peacetime.*

Eddy van Vliet Dutch
His poems appear frequently in Dutch journals.

Shelly Wagner American
Artist and poet, her poems have appeared in a number of journals including *American Poetry Review, Poetry East,* and *Bluff City;* her book of poems, *the Andrew Poems,* is winner of the Texas Tech University First Book Award.

Jeanne Murray Walker American
The author of a number of volumes of poetry including *Coming into History,* she was awarded the 1988 *Prairie Schooner*/Strousse Award for a sequence of poems about London; her first play, *Stories from 'The National Inquirer',* won the Washington D.C. National Theatre Competition.

Vernon Watkins Welsh
Author of a number of volumes of poems including *Affinities, The Death Bell,* and *Selected Poems 1930-1960,* he carried on correspondence with David Jones and Dylan Thomas, published as *David Jones: Letters to Vernon Watkins* and *Dylan Thomas: Letters to Vernon Watkins.*

Nancy Willard American
Poet, novelist, and essayist, her volumes of poetry include *Household Tales of Moon and Water, 19 Masks for the Naked Poet,* and *Carpenter and the Sun;* she won the Newbery Award for *A Visit to William Blake's Inn.*

Ellen Wittlinger American
Author of a book of poems, *Breakers,* her play, *The Deserving Rich,* was performed in Boston.

Judith Wright Australian
The recipient of numerous awards including the Encyclopaedia Britannica Writer's Award, she is a poet, essayist, and fiction writer; her poems appeared in a collected edition, *Collected Poems 1942-1970.*

Al Young American

He has recently served as Editor of *Believers,* a special issue of *Ploughshares,* which is a compilation of thirty-nine poets and nine fiction writers whose writings focus on the theme that to *believe* is to live.

Index of Poets

THE VIRAGO BOOK OF LOVE POETRY

Edited by Wendy Mulford

For centuries women have written about love with passion, humour, frustration and despair; but never before have their voices come together as in this exhilarating and timeless compendium. Here are love poems in all their true, subversive drama, delicately arranged according to a balance of moods and modes: of argument and lyric, joke and passionate utterance, rejection, rage and ecstasy.

Poets, well-known and obscure, ancient and modern – from Sappho to Akhmatova, Bessie Smith to Selima Hill, Sylvia Plath to Alice Walker – all challenge the traditional perception of woman as muse and object of desire, and magnificently transcend it.

THE VIRAGO BOOK OF WICKED VERSE

Edited by Jill Dawson

This wonderfully sharp and witty collection of poems – feisty, bawdy, erotic, irreverent – is an illuminating comment on women's ability to transform poetry into a medium of subversiveness. There are jibes at hyprocrisy and prejudice, plenty of sexiness and sauciness, and a riotous turning of the 'Lady Poet' image on its head ('A falling leaf could stir her. / A wilting, dying rose / would make her write, both day and night, / the most rewarding prose. / She'd find a hidden meaning / in every pair of pants / then hurry home to be alone / and write about romance' – *Maya Angelou*). With poets spanning continents and centuries, this anthology demonstrates lavishly the myriad ways in which women can be 'wicked' – by their definition – and wilfully so!

Poems by: Aphra Behn, Nina Cassian, Wendy Cope, Eunice de Souza, Emily Dickinson, Carol Ann Duffy, Lorna Goodison, Jackie Kay, Liz Lochhead, Suniti Namjoshi, Grace Nichols, Fiona Pitt-Kethley, Vicki Raymond, Ntozake Shange, Izumi Shikibu, Anna Wickham and many more.

VIRAGO NEW POETS

Edited by Melanie Silgardo

Virago proudly publish this volume of remarkable new poets. From the complex to the lyrical, their poetry excavates areas of doubt and ambivalence, joy and celebration as they suggest themes of sexuality, race, commitment, love, madness, relationships. With precision and fervour they each illuminate their poetry, and with wisdom and awareness, wit and sassiness, they stake their claim as the new generation of women poets. All featured here are as yet unpublished in solo volumes, but each has a substantial body of work. Many have been published in anthologies and journals and have won literary prizes.

BENEATH THE WIDE WIDE HEAVEN
Poetry of the environment from antiquity to the present

Edited by Sara Dunn with Alan Scholefield

In our time we have seen human response to our surroundings reach a seemingly unprecedented point of crisis; but as this anthology shows, the relationship between people and their environment has always been at the heart of poetry. For centuries poets have looked again 'beneath the wide wide heaven' – and have found beauty in unexpected places, or revealed surprising uneasiness that can be evoked by the most idyllic settings.

From the passionate to the angry, the urgent to the contemplative, the poems collected here constantly question and challenge, and encapsulate the extraordinarily complex and profound relationship between people and the places they inhabit.

Poems by: Anna Akhmatova, Gillian Allnutt, Elizabeth Bishop, Charlotte Brontë, C.P. Cavafy, Emily Dickinson, Michael Drayton, Helen Dunmore, Ruth Fainlight, Elaine Feinstein, U.A. Fanthorpe, Seamus Heaney, Nazim Hikmet, Gerard Manley Hopkins, Liz Lochhead, Hugh MacDiarmid, Antonio Machado, Charlotte Mew, Czeslaw Milosz, Pablo Neruda, Sylvia Plath, Stevie Smith, Alice Walker, Walt Whitman and others.

HARUKO/LOVE POETRY
New and Selected Love Poems

June Jordan

> 'June Jordan makes us think of Akhmatova, of Neruda.
> She is among the bravest of us, the most outraged . . .
> She is the universal poet'
> – Alice Walker

> 'Compassion, strength and determination is the hall mark of all
> Jordan's writing'
> – Margaret Busby

The joy, the erotic sweetness and the pain of love glow at the heart of this sensational volume of poetry. The Haruko poems dip and dovetail, taking from the haiku its purity and economy, but giving them a vision that is June Jordan's own. Every poem is a bud or bursting flower imbued with the most complex images as well as an aching desire to put right the whole Asian-American experience. Other poems selected from volumes published over the last twenty years bear witness to the depth and breadth of June Jordan's poetic brilliance. They bring to love poetry a new and more urgent definition.